How To Books

Living & Working in Britain

Living & Working in Britain

How to study, work and settle in the UK

CHRISTINE HALL
2nd edition

How To Books

By the same author in this series

How to Get a Job in Germany
How to Live & Work in Germany
How to Work in Retail (with Sylvia Lichfield)
Living and Working in China
Writing Features and Interviews

Published by How To Books Ltd,
3 Newtec Place, Magdalen Road,
Oxford OX4 1RE, United Kingdom.
Tel: (01865) 793806. Fax: (01865) 248780.
email: info@howtobooks.co.uk
www.howtobooks.co.uk

First published 1996
Second edition 2001

British Library Cataloguing in Publication Data
A catalogue record for this book is available from
the British Library

Cartoons by Mike Flanagan
Cover design by Shireen Nathoo Design
Cover image PhotoDisc

Produced for How To Books by Deer Park Productions
Typeset by PDQ Typesetting, Newcastle-under-Lyme, Staffs
Printed and bound in Great Britain by Bell & Bain Ltd, Glasgow

NOTE: The material contained in this book is set out in good
faith for general guidance and no liability can be accepted
for loss or expense incurred as a result of relying in particular
circumstances on statements made in the book. Laws and
regulations are complex and liable to change, and readers should
check the current position with the relevant authorities before
making personal arrangements.

Contents

List of Illustrations

Preface
to the second edition

At college in Germany, everyone talked about going to live and work abroad. I think I am the only one who really did it – and not before I was 25. All the others kept postponing the venture: 'I'll go to university first', 'Not now that my career is progressing', 'I'm just getting married', 'Too risky with a pregnant wife', 'Maybe when the children are older' were the excuses. Older people who had cherished similar dreams in their youth said, 'I'm too old for that sort of thing now . . . '. I guess one day they will say, 'I wish I had gone abroad when I was young'.

I chose Britain not because of my love for that country (don't tell the British!) but because it was the easiest solution. I knew the country from student holidays, spoke fluent English (or so I thought), and as a German national I did not require a work permit or a visa.

My first year was terrible: I found the British extremely reserved and was lonely. I couldn't get a job in my field as a journalist and had to work as a bilingual secretary instead.

I made all the mistakes a foreign girl can possibly make: I chatted to strangers on the London Underground (you must not talk to anyone to whom you have not been introduced). I discussed politics (the British enjoy complaining about their government but they dislike foreigners doing the same). I even jumped a queue in a bank (honestly, I didn't even notice there was a queue).

Eleven years later, I am happily settled in a small village in Kent. I have a wide circle of friends and earn a living as a freelance writer and adult education teacher. I have even learnt to eat toasted bread with salty butter and to drink tea with milk.

Is there something I would do differently, if I had the chance? Yes, I would prepare more carefully before going to Britain. But then I didn't have a book like this to help me. This book is for people who are in the same situation as I was, either planning to live and work in Britain, or already in the country and trying to survive those major and minor difficulties.

Please note that rules and regulations change constantly. Economic or political developments can have drastic effects on matters such as Social Security, National Health Service, and education. Telephone numbers, postal addresses, websites, contact names and fees change frequently too. Use the book as the starting point, but don't rely on it as your only source of information. Contact your embassy, the company, school, service provider or the local authorities for up-to-date advice.

The book shows Britain from a foreigner's perspective. It may be wise not to show it to British people. They are likely to disagree with some of the comments on British behaviour, and may find the sections on the British sense of humour not funny at all.

This book is dedicated to Monika Hägele and Thomas Borsch, fellow-aliens and survivors during my first year in England. Thanks also to everyone who helped me to settle in.

Many thanks to everyone who contributed their advice, information or experience to this book: Evelyn Thomsen and Christoph Neidlein and all my other friends in Germany who helped my venture with their encouragement and enthusiasm, and by storing my belongings and forwarding my mail. Also to the case study interviewees (some of whom have asked me to change their names and details to protect their identities), to the staff at the embassies and organisations, and the recruitment agents who agreed to be interviewed. For the second edition, I'd like to add special thanks to my new case study interviewees, Lynne Batik, Fiona Hodgson, Sigal Abbatovi, 'Zinga' Rabhi Abderrazak, Carina Westling.

If you have any comments or suggestions for future editions of this book, if you spot any errors or want to tell me about an organisation's change of address, please write to me c/o How To Books. I welcome your comments.

Christine Hall

1

Introducing Great Britain

LOOKING AT THE GEOGRAPHY

The United Kingdom of Great Britain and Northern Ireland is a nation of islands. The largest island is Great Britain, about 600 miles (900 kilometres) long from north to south. This large island includes England, Scotland and Wales, and is surrounded by smaller islands. The country is home to around 60,000,000 people.

The British will forgive a foreigner almost everything, but many will not if you refer to their country as England. The correct title is the United Kingdom of Great Britain and Northern Ireland. Great Britain, Britain, United Kingdom and UK are usually acceptable.

England, however, is only a small part of this kingdom, and the residents of Scotland, for example, take it as an insult to their national pride if you think them of them as English.

It is important that you differentiate between these parts of the country:

- England
- Wales
- Scotland
- Northern Ireland
- Channel Islands
- Isle of Man.

The main parts are divided into counties, administrative regions or districts. The names and borders of these counties varies depending on the purpose, which can be confusing. The place where you live may belong to one county for ceremonial purposes, to another one for administration matters, and yet another for postal delivery. What's more, the government changes the names and borders of the counties from time to time, uniting some counties into one, or creating another one, so take the list of counties and districts below with a pinch of salt. Most Britons don't understand the system either.

Fig. 1. Map of the UK.

England

England covers an area of about 130,000 square kilometres, and the capital is **London**. Forty-seven million people live in England. Their language is English. Their currency is the pound sterling (£), but they accept Scottish currency, too. The political status is that of a constitutional monarchy.

England is divided into counties: Avon, Bedfordshire, Berkshire, Buckinghamshire, Cambridgeshire, Cheshire, Cleveland, Cornwall, Cumbria, Derbyshire, Devon, Dorset, Durham, Essex, Gloucestershire, Greater London, Greater Manchester, Hampshire, Hereford and Worcester, Hertfordshire, Humberside, Isle of Wight, Kent, Lancashire, Leicestershire, Lincolnshire, Merseyside, Norfolk, Northamptonshire, Northumberland, Nottinghamshire, Oxford, Shropshire, Somerset, Staffordshire, Suffolk, Surrey, East Sussex, West Sussex, Tyne and Wear, Warwickshire, West Midlands, Wiltshire, North Yorkshire, South Yorkshire and West Yorkshire.

Scotland

Five and a quarter million people live in the 78,000 square kilometre area. The political status is a constitutional monarchy, and **Edinburgh** is the capital. Languages are English and Gaelic. The official currency is the Scottish pound sterling, but English money is equally accepted. The two currencies are interchangeable. Scotland has considerable administrative automony. The Scottish parliament is responsible for law, home affairs, education, training, church, local government, health, transport, social services, housing, economic development, environment, agriculture, fisheries, sports and the arts.

Scotland consists of several regions: Borders, Central, Dumfries and Galloway, Fife, Grampian, Highland, Lothian, Strathclyde, Tayside, Orkney Islands, Shetland Islands, Western Isles.

Wales

With 2.7 million people and 2,080 square kilometres in the west of the British mainland, the political status of Wales is that of a principality of Great Britain. The languages are English and Welsh, and the currency is the English pound sterling.

The counties of Wales are: Clwyd, Dyfed, Gwent, Gwynedd, Powys, Mid Glamorgan, South Glamorgan and West Glamorgan. Its principal city is **Cardiff**. The National Assembly for Wales is responsible for Welsh language, water, arts and heritage, industry, education and training, economic development, social services, agriculture and fisheries, environment, housing, health, highways, local government town and country planning and tourism.

The Channel Islands

The Channel Islands, of which Sark, Alderney, Guernsey and Jersey are the largest, lie near the French coast and are an autonomous democracy. They have their own parliament and even their own currency, and belong to Britain only in matters of foreign politics and defence.

Isle of Man

This island – also called 'Manx' – has its own parliament, currency and stamps, as well as tax laws favourable to the rich. It lies between the Lake District and Northern Ireland.

Northern Ireland

Northern Ireland (also called Ulster), with the capital **Belfast**, is part of the United Kingdom, but many of the people there don't like it if you call them British. As in other parts of the UK, there have been struggles for independence, and in Northern Ireland they have been fierce and often violent. Tread carefully.

The districts of Northern Ireland are: Antrim, Ards, Armagh, Ballymena, Ballymoney, Banbridge, Belfast, Carrickfergus, Castlereagh, Coleraine, Cookstown, Craigavon, Down, Dungannon, Fermanagh, Larne, Limavady, Lisburn, Londonderry, Magherafelt, Moyle, Newry and Mourne, Newtownabbey, North Down, Omagh and Strabane.

THE CLIMATE

Although the British climate is officially 'temperate', many visitors and immigrants find it unbearably cold and wet. The sky is overcast on more than half the days, and it rains frequently, especially in Scotland. Storm and floods occur often.

FOREIGN WORKERS

About two million foreigners live in Britain. That is about 3.6 per cent of the total population. A recently published survey estimates that 862,000 non-British nationals are working in this country – accounting for about 3.4 per cent of the total workforce.

If you decide to live and work in Britain, you won't be an unusual case. Especially in the cities, the British people live and work side by side with other nationals. The Labour Source Survey, published in the *Employment Gazette*, makes some remarkable observations:

* About 36,000 foreign nationals come to work in the UK every year.

* There are many nationals of the Irish Republic, India, Italy and the USA working in Britain.

* The foreign working population is on average more skilled than the local labour.

* Industries which are labour-intensive, especially distribution, hotels, catering and repairs, employ many foreigners.

* Most foreign nationals work in London and the immediate surroundings.

LOOKING AT ETHNIC MINORITIES

The British population is a melting pot of ethnic groups. Some have been assimilated, others prefer to live in separate quarters, forming their own communities. There are many Chinese, mostly from Hong Kong, Vietnamese, Indians (who often run corner shops or restaurants), Pakistanis, Bangladeshis, black West Indians, Arabs, and other groups.

This racial mix is partly the result of Britain's historical empire-building. On the whole, the British are tolerant of other people's ethnic background and customs. They don't mind the heavily veiled female bank clerk, or the Indian behind the railway ticket counter whose blue turban is carefully matched to his blue uniform. The British positively enjoy the variety of food which has been introduced by the ethnic groups. They try hard not to discriminate against anyone on grounds of ethnic origin.

However, problems may start if a British family find that their neighbourhood is gradually becoming a Pakistani, Arab, Chinese or whatever community – they may feel like aliens in their own country. Other critical situations arise when unemployed British nationals think that foreigners are taking the good jobs.

Don't refer to 'ethnic' people as 'English', even if they have a British passport and live in England. They won't mind, but some of the English (as in 'Anglo-Saxon') may get stroppy. But 'British' is safe.

EXPLORING BRITISH HISTORY

The history of Britain has been a history of invasions. Celts, Romans, Saxons, Vikings and Normans all conquered and occupied parts of the country. Later, Jews fleeing from the pogroms in central Europe, and people from the Commonwealth added to the racial mix.

Most Britons have little if any of the blood of the Briton tribe which gave its name to the country, or the Angles who gave their name to the English language.

Important dates

55 BC
This is the official date of the Roman invasion. In reality, it was only the date of one of Julius Caesar's raiding visits. The invasion began in 43 BC under Emperor Claudius. However, British pupils find it easier to remember '55' than '43'.

1066
The Battle of Hastings. The British regard this as the most important date in their history, because it was the last time anyone invaded Britain successfully, and the last time Britain lost a war. The English king Harold and his soldiers marched from the north of England, where they had just beaten Viking would-be invaders, to the south coast, where the French (Normans) prepared an invasion.

Both Kind Harold and the Duke of Normandy (later known as William the Conqueror) claimed that the previous king had nominated them as his successor, ignoring the fact that the king wouldn't have had the right to choose his own successor anyway. The question is complex, and British historians still enjoy discussing its aspects.

1529
King Henry VIII became head of the English Church. There were many political reasons for this, but the British like to imagine he

broke with the Catholic church to be able to divorce and remarry whenever he fancied a change of wives.

1588
The Spanish fleet, the Armada, tried to invade England.

1603
James I (and VI of Scotland) united the English and Scottish crowns.

1649
King Charles I was executed during the Civil War after arguments with parliament over the usual matters politicians argue about: taxes. foreign politics, religion and so on. The British never got over the sacrilege they had committed and in 1660 put his son on the throne as Charles II, so they had a monarchy with all its problems as before. The 11 years between 1649 and the restoration of the monarchy saw Britain governed by the non-monarchial system known as the Commonwealth.

1666
The great Fire of London destroyed much of the city. The Londoners result a more modern, safer town, and this gave the famous architect Christopher Wren a marvellous opportunity to display his skills. The main reason why the British like this date is that it's easy to remember.

1914–18
World Word I: The British Empire, France and Russia against Germany, Austria-Hungary and their allies.

1920
The Home Rule Act incorporated the north-east of Ireland (Ulster) into the United Kingdom of Great Britain and Northern Ireland.

1939–1945
World War II: Britain, the Commonwealth, France, the USA, the USSR and China against Germany, Italy and Japan. Note: This is one of the few occasions when the British (or English, depending on how far back you go in history) and the French fought on the same side. Previously the British (English) and the French spent their time mostly fighting each other.

1961
Britain applied unsuccessfully to join the EEC (European Economic Community). The British repeated their application in 1969, and finally succeeded in 1973. Since then they have been debating if and how they could get out again.

1997–2000
Devolution of Scotland and Wales. Constitutional changes to give Scotland and Wales greater autonomy. The changes were drastic but gradual and peaceful. The Britons wonder from time to time why the question of Northern Ireland independence cannot be solved in the same way instead of street fights in Belfast and bomb explosions in London.

UNDERSTANDING POLITICS

The parliament
The British parliament consists of two sections: The House of Commons and the House of Lords. Members of the House of Commons are elected by the people and called MPs (Members of Parliament). If someone has a problem or cause which they think deserves wider attention, they contact their MP who will, if necessary, bring the matter up in the House of Commons. The person presiding over the House of Commons is the Speaker.

Members of the House of Lords are all Lords and Ladies, either hereditary peers or life peers. There are also Law Lords (judges) and Spiritual Peers (bishops). The Lord Chancellor presides over the House of Commons.

You can watch the debates in the House of Commons and the House of Lords as a visitor.

Political parties
The major parties in Great Britain are Conservative (also called the Tories), Labour and Liberal Democrat (successor to the Whig party).There are several smaller and mainly nationalistic groups such as the Scottish National Party.

The Prime Minister
The Prime Minister is the head of the government. He or she must be a member of the House of Commons and is normally the leader of the political party which won most seats in the House at general

election time, although minority governments have been known.

The cabinet
This is a committee of ministers, selected by the prime minister, which forms the main engine of government.

Government information
You can write to government departments and ask them to explain how something is done, or why. There is even a brochure called *Open Government* which contains the address and contact names of government departments. It also includes a form which you can photocopy and send to the relevant department.

You will get an answer within 21 days. The information is normally free. If it involves much work, you will be asked if you are willing to pay a charge. You can order the brochure from (enclose a stamped addressed envelope): Open Government, Room 417b, Office of Public Service, 70 Whitehall, London SW1A 2AS.

For addresses of government departments, see the Useful Addresses section.

Royalty
British is a parliamentary monarchy. The monarch – currently Queen Elizabeth II – has no real power. She reigns, but she does not govern. Her contribution to British politics is mostly titular.

Other members of the royal family also perform a representative role at home and overseas: shaking hands, smiling, visiting hospitals and old people's homes, cutting ribbons, unveiling plaques and planting trees. The newspapers and magazines discuss their private lives, and the British enjoy gossiping about them. The main complaints are that Royals don't lead strictly moral lives and that they get too much money.

You can discuss the royal family freely, as long as you don't criticise the Queen or the Queen Mother. They are sacrosanct.

Your right to vote
If you come to live in the UK, you will possibly lose your right to vote in your home country. It is likely that you will not gain the right to vote in Britain instead. This can be frustrating if you are politically-minded. However, some foreign nationals may vote in certain elections while they are resident in the UK.

- Citizens of Commonwealth countries and citizens of the Irish Republic may vote in parliamentary, European parliamentary and local government elections.

- European Union citizens can vote at European parliamentary elections, but not in UK parliamentary elections. There will probably be changes soon, allowing you to vote at local government elections.

- Citizens of other countries cannot vote in the UK at any level. There are no plans to change this.

If you want more information about your right to vote, contact the Home Office, Queen Anne's Gate, London SW1H 9AT.

OBSERVING THE LAW

Once in the UK, you are subject to the laws of the UK. You have to obey them whether you like them or not.

If you need legal advice, one option is to go to a **solicitor**, which can be expensive as solicitors charge high fees. If you need the services of a solicitor and live on a very low income, you may be entitled to legal aid.

Alternatively, you can visit your nearest **Citizens Advice Bureau**, found in most towns. The volunteers working there are not solicitors, but volunteers with some legal training. They can tell you if something you want to do is right or wrong, or if they are any pitfalls. They will advise you what to do if you are in a difficult situation. But they will not represent your case or defend you in court.

You don't need an appointment; just go to the office during opening hours. You may have to wait a few minutes until someone is free to see you. The advice is free, and you don't have to be poor to seek their help. But if you can afford it, you can leave a small donation, as the CAB operates on a limited budget.

If you are in serious trouble (for example, if you get arrested by the police and don't understand why), contact your country's **embassy** or high commission in Britain.

Exploring Britain on the Internet
The following sites contain useful links:

http://www.mistral.co.uk/hammerwood/uk.htm
http://www.visitbritain.com
http://www.great-britain.co.uk/
http://www.westken.dircon.co.uk/bearpage/babctour/htm

CASE STUDIES

Fiona finds Scotland dark

'I was training horses and studying at home in Australia. Britain was always the first place I wanted to see, you are so central to travel to all the other countries if you base yourself in Britain. What did strike me most on arrival in Lockerbie in Scotland in December, was the darkness. Nothing could have prepared me for that. The darkness is at its worst in December. The other thing I noted about the scenery is the greenness of everything.'

Zinga hates the weather

'Compared with the climate in Tunisia, the British weather is so horrible and miserable that I often wish I was not here.'

2

Getting into Britain

FOLLOWING IMMIGRATION PROCEDURE

The immigration procedure is complex, and details may change at short notice. This chapter will give you the information you need to start making plans. However, you must get full and up-to-date information before you take any decisions.

The place to contact is the British embassy or high commission in your country. They have different leaflets for the various purposes of stay available and update them constantly. They can also send you visa application and other relevant forms.

European nationals

Immigration is easy for **EU** and **EEA** nationals. You are free to enter the UK for up to six months to look for work or set up in business. You can continue looking for a job indefinitely, but you may have to prove that you are genuinely job-hunting and that you have realistic prospects of finding work.

You don't need a work permit. A British employer can employ you just like a British national. You don't even need a residence permit, although you may apply for one if you wish once you have found work. Use the form ECC1, available from The Immigration and Nationality Department, European Community Group, B6 Division, Lunar House, 40 Wellesley Road, Croydon CR9 2BY.

Other nationals

Before coming into the UK, you must get entry clearance. Depending on your nationality, one of the following is necessary:

- **entry certificate** (mostly for nationals of Commonwealth countries)

- **letter of consent** (for nationals of non-Commonwealth, non-visa countries)

- **visa** (for nationals of all other countries, referred to as 'visa countries').

If you are from a country whose nationals must get a **visa**, don't even think about arriving without one: the authorities will send you home at your own expense.

People from other countries apply for 'leave to enter' as a visitor when they come through British immigration control. You will need your passport, proof of enough money to finance your stay, and evidence of the purpose of your stay. However, they may reject you – what then?

Please note that the visa countries list is changed often. It is important to get the latest information from the British embassy or high commission in your country on which type of entry clearance you need, and apply for it at an early stage.

The entry clearance will also depend on the purpose of your stay. There are several categories:

As a visitor
Your visa will probably have a limit of six months, and may have to specify what the purpose of your visit is, for example, to visit a relative.

To study
You may be asked to produce written confirmation from the school, college or university. You can find detailed advice in the book *How to Study & Live in Britain*.

To work
You will probably need a work permit, as well as proof of employment (see below).

To set up your own business
You will have to prove that you have the necessary capital (currently £200,000).

Applying for political asylum
You will have to prove to the Home Office that you would be persecuted in your country because of your race, religion, nationality, membership of a particular social group or political opinion. It is difficult to get asylum in Britain.

You will have to pay a fee for your entry clearance, whatever the purpose of your stay.

Getting a work permit

If you apply for, and find, a job in Britain while you are still in your country, your employers must apply to the Employment Department for permission to employ you. They may have to prove that there was no other suitable candidate, and that your skills, experience and qualifications are necessary. There are many highly skilled foreign workers in the UK. If you don't have good skills, or if your skills are in a type of job for which there is a high unemployment rate, you may not get a work permit.

Some people don't need work permits for their jobs: missionaries, ministers of religion, sole representatives of overseas firms and servants of diplomats. Artists and writers may carry out their work as long as they don't take on other jobs.

Young Commonwealth citizens

If you are a Commonwealth citizen aged between 17 and 27, you can come to the UK for a working holiday for up to two years. You must be able to prove that you don't need public funds for your stay and that you have enough money to pay for your return journey. Your work must be 'incidental' to your holiday. To prove this, you may have to show that you do a lot of sightseeing and take on only casual jobs. Many young people from Australia, New Zealand and Canada use this option freely already; it is less known among other Commonwealth citizens.

Joining your partner

If your husband, wife, fiancé or fiancée is already living in the UK, you may be allowed to join them. There are several conditions attached:

- You must know your partner personally. This is particularly important if yours is an arranged marriage. You don't need to prove that you know each other well, or that you had contact after the betrothal was arranged. This is to prevent problems such as 'mail order brides' and hidden slavery.

    It may be enough that you used to play together as children, or that you were introduced to each other before the betrothal. But you must both remember it. A photo showing you and your partner is obvious evidence.

- You plan to live together permanently as husband and wife. It is not enough to go through a legal form of marriage.

- You didn't get married just to be allowed into the UK. If you have been married for at least five years, or if you have a child from this marriage, the authorities will usually be satisfied. Otherwise you may have to show that you had a good reason to get married – for example, love. In this case, love letters can be useful evidence.

- There will be suitable accommodation for you, your husband or wife, and your dependants.

- You and your husband or wife can support yourselves and don't need to use public funds. This means that between you, you must earn or own enough money to feed, clothe and house your family.

You have to apply yourself. Your partner cannot do this for you. You will have to pay an application fee, which is currently £80.

The forms are available from the British high commission or embassy in your home country. You can also get them from the Migration and Visa Department, Foreign and Commonwealth Office, Clive House, Petty France, London SW1H 9HD.

It can take several months until you are invited for an interview, especially if you come from the Indian subcontinent, Jamaica, the Philippines or Thailand. At the interview, you need many documents to prove that you can meet all the above conditions. Never present false documents or certificates, they will only lead you into trouble. If a particular document does not exist, simply explain this, and there may be a way around it. For example, if a marriage certificate is not issued in your country, the British high commission may accept declarations from your and your partner's family.

Procedures are simpler if you are married to an EU citizen who is working or studying in the UK, or if you are a female Commonwealth citizen married to a male British citizen. You may not need more than a certificate of entitlement to the right of abode. Get in touch with the British embassy or high commission in your home country about this.

For more information, obtain the Immigration Fact Sheet 1 from the Joint Committee for the Welfare of Immigrants (JCWI) (see Useful Addresses).

Joining your child or grandchild

If your son, daughter or grandchild is already living in the UK, you may be allowed to join them. You must show that you are depending financially on your child, and that you have no close relatives in your country to whom you could turn. You must be 65 or over. You must apply before you enter the country. You can get the relevant forms from your nearest British embassy or high commission. If you succeed, you have to pay a fee, currently £145.

You may find the Immigration Fact Sheet 1 from the JCWI useful (see Useful Addresses).

Getting your children to join you

If you are settled in the UK, and have unmarried children under 18 whom you can support and accommodate, you can sponsor them to join you in the UK. Application forms are available from the Migration and Visa Department, Foreign and Commonwealth Office, Clive House, Petty France, London SW1H 9HD.

Further details are explained in the Immigration Fact Sheet 2 from the JCWI.

Extending a visitor visa

Visitor visas are usually valid for six months. Once you are in the country, you can apply for an extension to the Immigration and Nationality Department, Home Office, Lunar House, Wellesley Road, Croydon CR9 2BY. However, such extensions are often refused.

REGISTERING WITH THE POLICE

You should register with the police within seven days after arrival, unless you are an EU or Commonwealth national. Registration may also be waived in some other circumstances, but these may change. It is safest to report to the nearest police station and offer to register.

Some embassies in London also keep a register of nationals of their country. Phone your embassy shortly after you arrive and ask if they would like your details.

THE JOINT COUNCIL FOR THE WELFARE OF IMMIGRANTS

Since 1967 the JCWI has been the only national independent voluntary organisation which specialises in British immigration and nationality law. It provides advice for individuals, families and groups from Britain's minority ethnic communities who visit or write to the office. It also provides up-to-date information on changes to the law, the rules and their implementation. The JCWI campaigns against racism and injustice in immigration and nationality law.

For immigrants, the most useful service is the availability of **fact** and **advice leaflets**. These leaflets can help you with specific problems or queries. The JCWI makes a small charge for these to cover costs.

You can also become a member of the JCWI for an annual fee of £20. For more information about membership and information services, contact the Joint Council for the Welfare of Immigrants, 115 Old Street, London EC1V 9JR.

PAYING CUSTOMS DUTY

When you arrive at the airport you have to take your luggage through a customs channel. There are two channels.

The green channel
Use the green channel if you are sure that you have **no goods to declare**. European Union nationals can almost always use the green channel. You will walk past customs officials who look at everyone carefully. They may ask you to open your luggage and prove that you have no goods to declare. They ask everyone who looks or acts suspicious. But they also ask many average travellers, simply because they have to do spot checks. This does not reflect badly on you. Just be polite, allow them to search your suitcases. Never try to cheat by taking the green channel when you have something to declare. This would make you a smuggler. You don't want to start your stay in the UK as a criminal, do you?

The red channel
The red channel means **goods to declare**. You use it if you are carrying more than your allowance of duty and tax free goods or if you carry any goods which are not normally allowed from your country into the UK. You may have to pay customs (import tax). If you are in any doubt which channel to choose, take the red one and ask the customs officials there.

If you move to live in the UK and have a work permit or have enrolled for a full-time course of study, you can bring your personal belongings such as clothes, furniture and household linen as long as you have used them for several months outside the UK. You won't have to pay customs duty for them.

Contact the British embassy or high commission in your home

country to find out what you may or may not bring to the UK. Forbidden items include:

- many drugs (such as opium and heroin)
- most animals (alive or dead)
- products made from protected species (ivory jewellery, crocodile leather handbags)
- some horror and pornographic books, comics, videos etc
- most meat and meat products, and some fish
- certain plants
- non-approved radio transmitters and cordless telephones.

If in doubt, ask before you bring the items into the UK. Never agree to take luggage or parcels for other people from your country to the UK. They may contain smuggled or prohibited goods and could get you into deep trouble.

TAKING YOUR PET WITH YOU

Britain has strict **quarantine** regulations for animals. This is to keep rabies and other diseases out of the country. If you want to bring your pet into the UK, it involves so much time, trouble and money that it may be better to leave the animal behind. A new scheme called PETS (pet travel scheme) now allows you to bring your dog or cat with you, if you and your pet come from a country approved by DEFRA (Department for Environment, Food and Rural Affairs). To qualify, your cat or dog must:

- be fitted with a microchip
- be vaccinated against rabies
- be blood tested
- be issued with an official PETS certificate
- be treated against tapeworm and ticks.

The countries currently taking part in the scheme are: Andorra, Austria, Belgium, Denmark, Finland, France, Germany, Gibraltar, Greece, Iceland, Italy, Liechtenstein, Luxembourg, Monaco, the Netherlands, Norway, Portugal, San Marino, Spain, Sweden, Switzerland and the Vatican.

If your pet does not qualify, expect to fill in many forms before you get a licence to import it. You must have a confirmed booking for your pet at an approved kennel, you must use the services of an authorised carrying agent, and the animal must arrive at an approved airport or seaport. Then your pet must stay for several months in 'quarantine' at the kennel. The length of the quarantine depends on the animal. The quarantine period can be a lonely and desperate experience for your pet, although you may visit it.

The procedure is costly: expect to pay about £750 for a dog's quarantine accommodation alone – and this does not include the costs for transport, vaccinations and certificates.

Don't even think about smuggling your pet into the country. It will inevitably be found and be put down, and you will end up in prison and have to pay a hefty fine.

If you want to bring an animal to the UK, contact DEFRA for details of the PETS scheme, for lists of kennels, application forms and the latest regulations. Their website is comprehensive and user-friendly.

Department for Environment, Food and Rural Affairs, Hook Rise South, Tolworth, Surbiton, Surrey, KT6 7NF. Tel: 0870 241 1710, e-mail: *pets@ahvg.maff.gsi.gov.uk www.maff.gov.uk/animals/quarantine*

CHECKLIST

1. Am I clear about the purpose of my stay?

2. How long do I plan to stay?

3. Have I written to the British embassy (or high commission) to get definite information on what the immigration procedure would be for me?

4. Do I plan to work in the UK? Does my work require a work permit?

5. Am I planning to go alone, or with my family?

6. Do I have family in the UK? If yes, could I apply to join them?

7. Do I have all the relevant documents ready?

8. Have I applied for entry clearance or for permission to join my

family in the UK?

9. How long is it likely to take to get entry clearance?

10. If I go to the UK as a visitor, do I have enough money to support me during my stay and the return ticket?

11. Do I want to take on work while I'm in the UK? Am I allowed to (for example, working holidays for young Commonwealth citizens, or holders of work permits)?

CASE STUDIES

Laurenz leaves home

'I was 18 and desperate to get away from my family in Paris. Like many teenagers, I didn't get on with my parents and longed for adventure. I wanted to go to America, if possible to New York. I signed up with an au pair agency, and they found me a placement. But then the American embassy in Paris refused to give me a visa. I have never found out why.

'By that time, I was so keen on going abroad that when the agency suggested I could become an au pair in another country I agreed. It would have to be a European country because I did not want to risk any more delays because of visas. I thought my English was better than my German, so I asked to be posted to Britain. I came for a year – but that was eight years ago. I'm happily married to an Englishman and we have twin boys. I feel more English than French.'

Caroline finds it easy

'Arriving in Britain to look for work was no different from my previous stays as a tourist. I showed my Belgian passport, walked through the green channel, and took the underground train to the cheap hotel where I had booked accommodation for the first week.

'I thought I would have to go through a complicated procedure, but it was as if I were British myself. I registered with a bilingual secretarial employment agency. The consultant there had dealt with European Union applicants before and told me that I didn't even need a work permit. I was almost disappointed how easy it all was.'

Andrew leaves his dog behind

'The dog I had in Canada was such a gregarious creature. He would have been so unhappy during the six months' quarantine. And, being used to the countryside, he probably wouldn't have enjoyed life in London at all. Luckily my sister agreed to take him. This meant a new home, but with a familiar person. She took some of my furniture too, so there were a few items he recognised. He settled in well, although he was disturbed for the first few months. I know he is in good hands, and he has accepted my sister as his new leader. But when I visited the USA, he was crazy with joy at seeing me again. He must have thought I was dead.'

Monica stays by accident

'I am Korean, and I came to live in Britain by accident. If I had chosen a country to live in, I would have gone to some adventurous place, like Egypt or Brazil. At the time, I was doing meditation studies in India. My visa for India ran out, and I had to go to another country while applying for a new visa so that I could continue my studies.

'Britain was the easiest. I thought I was going to stay for just a few days or weeks. By the time I realised that my visa for India would not be renewed, I had come to like Britain. So I stayed.'

Ling joins her fiancé

'I met my British husband when he spent four years in southern China as an English teacher at the college in my home town. We got engaged just before he left for home, but it took more than a year until I could follow him.

'To be honest, it was more difficult to get permission to leave China than to get into the UK! There was an incredible amount of paperwork before I was given a Chinese passport.

'At the British embassy, I had to prove that I really knew George. This was no problem, because we had been colleagues for several years. I was also interviewed about our relationship. The officer wanted to make sure that I didn't marry him just to get entry clearance to the UK. Many colleagues and friends had offered to testify that ours was a real love relationship, but it was not necessary. The way I talked about George convinced the officials. One obstacle occurred when George didn't find a job at once, and did therefore not have enough income to support us. In the end, his parents guaranteed that they would feed me until George and I found jobs.'

Mansour produces letters from his bride

'When I applied to join my fiancée in the UK, the authorities thought our engagement was just a pretence, especially as I admitted freely that ours was to be an arranged Iranian marriage. They found it difficult to believe that a young man could be truly fond of a girl whom his parents had selected for him, and whom he had not seen for several years. They asked me what I liked about Marjam, and smiled when I praised her small hands, her embroidery skills and her cookery. These were obviously not qualities the British men look for in their brides.

'I had to tell our story again and again. I explained how I had asked my mother to introduce a suitable girl, how carefully the two families considered our personalities, how we visited her and her family, how she and I talked privately for a few minutes and gladly agreed to a betrothal, and how we met a couple of times afterwards. We hoped to get married soon, but then her family went to Europe, and I completed my education in Iran. Marjam's career in England was progressing well, and she did not wish to leave her parents. I was more ready for a change of environment.

'Luckily my memories of our few meetings were detailed, and I had kept Marjam's occasional letters from London. Of course her letters were not what you would call love letters, more the sort of letter a girl would write to an elder brother. But they were sufficient to prove that we knew and were fond of each other.'

Lynne falls in love

'I am American and was studying history, and came to Scotland for my 'Junior Year Abroad' exercise for university, because British history has always interested me. The paperwork for a year studying here was mostly internal bureaucracy for the universities involved. For the UK government I had to fill in only a single immigration form, the one designed for the granting of student visas.

'While I was here I fell in love with a native Aberdonian...and that, as they say, was that. I returned to the US for a year to complete my degree, and then moved back to Aberdeen specifically to marry Allan.

'This time I came over on a fiancée visa, which is for three months, does not allow you to work, and requires that you marry the specified UK citizen in a legally recognised ceremony within that time. There was a considerable stack of paperwork associated with this, involving documenting who we were, how we had met, our history of contact (to prove that our marriage wasn't a fraudulent pretence), as well as our savings and financial status, criminal history and all those other multitudinous things governments want to know about you.

'If we had married first and then applied, the stack of paperwork would have been even bigger.

'After the wedding, we sent proof of the ceremony and my passport to the Home Office, and they stamped the passport for a one-year provisional residency. Now I was allowed to work without restriction, had to pay UK taxes, but was not allowed to draw any UK governmental benefits. Unfortunately, this also affected my husband's benefits; he lost his housing support benefit.

'After I had managed to support myself for a year, not gotten in trouble with the police and otherwise proven that I was a desirable person to have in the country, I sent a new set of forms, tax forms as proof of employment, and testimony that I was still married, off to the Home Office with my passport again, and this time they gave me an embossed stamp for unrestricted permanent residency. This allows me to do everything except vote here.'

Fiona finds the paperwork acceptable
'As an Australian, I had to complete all the paperwork for my passport and working visa. It was a lot, but all relevant. Then I had to fill in a tiny form on the plane, but once I arrived I didn't have to do any more paperwork.'

Sigal loves London
'I had just completed my last year at school in Australia. I came to London with the intention of working here for two months, then going travelling in Europe and the USA, returning home and starting my university degree. I just had to prove that I had more than AU$5000, and send my passport away for three months, no big deal.

'I fell in love with London to the extent that I wanted to stay here. I thought about studying here, and it was a quick decision.'

Zinga gets frustrated by the formalities
'My wife is British and it was her idea that we should live in England rather than Tunisia. For my visa application I had to provide a passport, a job identification, a bank statement, a rent contract, my wife's passport, her bank statement, an application form and £270. It was complicated to prove the rent contract. So my wife and I separated for two months, just so that she could live in England to

establish a rent contract. The interview at the British Embassy was annoying. I felt I was being investigated and cross-questioned as a crime suspect.'

Carina studies and stays

'After working in my home country in Sweden for seven years, I wanted to experience what it would be like to actually live in another country. I wanted to pursue dance and also look deeper into another art form, calligraphy. I moved to London and studied there for three years. I moved into a house where most people were working with performance one way or another, so friends and contacts grew from there. In London I met my husband. Together, we travelled the world for a couple of years. On return, we didn't want to settle in London, or anywhere else we'd already lived. We knew Brighton on the South coast had a reputation for being a friendly, cosmopolitan and interesting place to live. We decided to give it a go and grew to love it, and here we still are, six years later.'

POINTS TO CONSIDER

1. If you plan to, and are allowed to, work in the UK, for example as a young Commonwealth citizen on a working holiday or as a freelance artist, what will you do if you don't earn any money?

2. What will you do if the employer who promised to get you a work permit can't get one?

3. If you plan to stay with relatives as a visitor, or to join family members permanently, are you sure they want to have you with them?

4. What is the better for your pet: to stay behind, or to come with you? Look at all the pros and cons from the animal's point of view.

5. How will you feel if officials probe deeply into the nature of your relationship with your spouse or betrothed?

3

Understanding the British

BEING A FOREIGNER

Your first few months in Britain will be a time of readjustment. You will gradually get used to the British way of life.

You will have embarrassing, painful and frustrating experiences, even if they seem funny a few years later. For every time you think 'I like the way the British do this' there will be an occasion when you sigh 'Why can't they do it the same as in my country?'

While you learn to understand the British, you will also learn to understand your own culture and learn about yourself, how you respond to pressure and difficulties.

If possible, spend a holiday with a host family in Britain before you come to live here. The culture shock will be less severe.

Meeting prejudice and tolerance

Luckily, the British are more tolerant than most other people about foreigners, their habits and lifestyles. Especially in the cities they are used to living and working side by side with many different nationalities. You will rarely meet open hostility because of your race or creed.

This tolerance is because of the history of the British Empire, which embraced people of so many different nationalities, and because many British people served in the army in the colonies and learnt about different lifestyles.

The only infuriating aspect about this tolerance is that it can be slightly condescending. The British are kind to foreigners, but think they themselves are superior. Some seem to expect constant gratitude and admiration. The British have not fully realised that they lost their empire long ago – or if they are aware of it, they seem to long secretly to get it back. Some people say that the British only joined the European Community because they thought they could rule Europe instead and expected that everyone in those slightly inferior continental countries would look up at them in admiration.

Occasionally, problems may flare up if British (as in white Anglo-Saxon) people have been made redundant and see that you, as a newly arrived foreigner, hold a good, well-paid job. They may get the impression (probably wrongly) that you are taking away their jobs.

Another potential problem arises when a certain area attracts more and more people of a particular nationality. The British people who have lived there for a long time may feel they are suddenly transferred from their familiar neighbourhood into Chinatown and resent this.

The British may be alarmed if there is an assembly of more than two foreigners of any one nationality on British ground. They may even forget their good manners.

BECOMING SNOWED IN

When it snows, everything comes to a halt. If the snow is deeper than about an inch, schools send the children home, banks and libraries close, buses and trains get cancelled. There is a general feeling of panic.

Every four years or so there is a 'severe' winter with heavy snowfalls. You would think that the British would be prepared for this. But no. Each time they behave as if they were facing a disaster on the scale of an earthquake.

They start buying up all the bread and milk in the shop, hoarding supplies at home which would feed their families for months (although the average 'severe' winter lasts for a couple of weeks only). As a result, you can't buy any bread or milk in the shops.

Making preparations

It's a good idea for you to prepare yourself for the case of a 'severe' winter: keep some long life milk and a few packets of crisp bread under your bed. This is not because of the danger of real food shortage, but because the British panic may create artificial shortages.

You would also think that if other countries with heavier snowfalls manage to keep their public transport system up and their cars going, the British would be able to do the same. They don't. Their vehicles don't even have winter tyres which would, in another country, be routinely fitted at the beginning of winter.

Many houses are equally ill-equipped for winter. Water and drainage pipes are often unprotected on the outside of the house. They may freeze – so you won't get any running water and can't flush the toilet. They may burst – and then you're in serious trouble.

If there is heavy snow, the British don't go to work. Depending on your employers, you may be asked to take work home, or you have to use some of your holiday entitlement. But many employers don't expect their staff to come to work if it snows, and give them the time off. Ask your employers what their policy is.

SUPPORTING CHARITIES

A great deal of social life in Britain seems to revolve around **charities**. Fundraising events provide much entertainment. There are fundraising dinner-dances, cabarets, concerts, coffee mornings and jumble sales. The profits from these events go towards a particular charity – anything from cancer research to a donkey sanctuary.

Many people do weird things in the name of a charity. Often, this is a good excuse for otherwise reserved, correct people to behave crazily. 'It's for charity' is an acceptable excuse for almost everything.

This is how it works: A colleague walks from one department to another, carrying a list. 'I'm raising funds for a retirement stable for old race horses. How much money will you give me if I do a bungee jump from 120 metres?'

You can't really say no, so you promise to pay her, say, £1 if she does it. She asks you to write your promise in your list. She does her jump, you give her the money. If one hundred people offered to pay £1 each, and if the jump cost £50, she makes £50 profit which she gives to a charity.

Certain charities try to persuade everyone into giving money on certain days every year. For example, they ask you to pay for a red plastic nose (the money minus the manufacturing cost goes to the charity). Then, on the appointed day, people all over the UK are expected to wear a plastic nose on their face when they go to work.

They try to make you feel a miserly outsider if you are the only one in your college, company or village who is not wearing a red nose. But take heart: even some British people refuse to join in this so-called fun, so you need not feel guilty if you find this ridiculous.

It gets worse. They even sell large red plastic noses for cars (trying to make you feel guilty if you are the owner of the only noseless vehicle in the car park), and have recently introduced giant red plastic noses for buildings. Just to make sure that nobody gets away with reusing last year's nose, there is a slightly different design every year.

SLIMMING AND KEEP FIT

Many British people (especially women) are obsessed with losing weight and keeping fit. There are many magazines dedicated to slimming and/or keep fit. There are also lots of instructional videos on which a superslim, superfit woman demonstrates exercises for a slim tummy. She has probably achieved her flat tummy and narrow waist by rib removal and liposuction, but this is not the point. The average British woman won't do the exercises anyway. She feels she has done enough by buying a video, studying the low calorie recipes, subscribing to a slimming magazine. Occasionally they may start a weightloss diet and exercise programme, but they rarely complete it.

HAVING TEA

Tea can be something to drink or something to eat. It depends on the place, the time and the people.

If you have tea in the office, it is generally a hot drink in a paper cup from a vending machine.

You may have tea in a café, or in the home of a (middle or upper-class) friend or neighbour, at about 4pm. This will be either a platter of dainty cucumber and shrimp sandwiches (with the crust removed, if upper class), or two small cakes, crumpets or scones per person, probably with butter or jam. There will also be a pot of tea.

If you have tea with somebody's family (especially working or lower middle class) after 6pm, it is a simple hot or cold meal. You may or may not get tea to drink with it. If a colleague says at the end of the working day 'I have to buy my tea', she'll probably leave the shop carrying bread and vegetables or a frozen ready meal, maybe a can of beer, but no tea.

You can prepare tea (the drink) with tea bags or with loose leaves. Unlike teas in other countries, most British teas need to be immersed in boiling water for only a few seconds. Leave it longer and it is too strong. If you prepare tea in a teapot, you leave the tea bags in the pot, and each time you fill the cups you pour more hot water into the pot.

The British generally drink their tea diluted with milk. You may find this custom barbaric, spoiling the delicate flavour of the tea. But once you have tried British tea bags, you'll understand.

You drink tea either from cups or from mugs. Cups with matching saucers are used if a group of people are sitting down on a formal occasion. If you drink tea on your own, or with a neighbour, daughter or colleague, you use mugs. Mugs are much larger, and often decorated with silly pictures and comments. People like to give them as presents. Buy your own mug (or use that ridiculous thing someone gave you for Christmas) to use at your workplace.

BEING VEGETARIAN

About ten per cent of all British people are full- or part-time vegetarians. However, estimates vary, depending on whether it's a meat producer or a manufacturer of vegetarian meals who pays for the survey.

Every restaurant, down to the smallest pub, has at least one vegetarian dish on the menu. Unfortunately, it's almost always 'vegetarian lasagne' and you'll get bored with it.

It is fashionable to be vegetarian, and many teenage girls become vegetarians for a few months until they give in to the temptation of a big beefburger.

If you are invited to a meal, just mention that you are a vegetarian, and your host, hostess or chef will arrange something for you. If you are organising a meal, it is important to ask 'Are any of you vegetarians?' or (in a letter or form) 'Please say here if you have special dietary requirements'.

Vegetarians don't eat dead (or living) animals, but they consume animal products that don't involve an animal's death: eggs (preferably free-range), milk, butter, yoghurt.

Being a **vegan**, or catering for one, is more complicated: they won't eat anything made from animal products at all.

There are also a lot of part-time vegetarians who eat meat only occasionally, or they eat only white meat, or only fish.

There are magazines dedicated to the interests of vegetarians and vegans.

COUNSELLING

Many love stories in British women's magazines have a modern happy ending: the violent husband and the jealous wife take counselling, realise their faults, amend their behaviour and live happily forever after.

If you have a problem and don't have anyone with whom you can talk things over, you can pay someone to listen to you. These people are trained and qualified counsellors. They won't give you advice –

they will just keep you talking for an hour at a time, for weeks, until you have found your own solutions.

Counselling can be a real help especially with emotional or repressed problems, and there is no stigma attached to taking counselling. Counselling is good for you. (I would say so, of course, as I hold two qualifications in basic counselling skills.)

The problem is that a single counselling session won't usually solve your problem. You'll need a whole string of sessions, and they are expensive. Expect to pay about £30 for each session.

If you need someone to talk to, but can't afford to pay a professional counsellor, phone or visit the nation-wide network of Samaritans. They provide counselling for free. You don't have to be on the brink of suicide: they are ready to help everyone. The volunteers are not usually fully qualified counsellors, but they are trained in basic counselling skills.

Alternatively, just find a sympathetic person who knows how to listen without interrupting.

'SO SORRY!'

The British say 'please', 'thank you' and 'I'm sorry' all the time. They will never order someone to do something: they phrase every order as a polite request. For example, the boss will ask her secretary: 'Jane, would you mind filing this pile of letters for me?' But it is an order nevertheless, and the secretary can't say 'Yes, I would mind.'

Protests and criticism are phrased as questions, polite and slightly apologetic. 'Would you mind awfully if I asked you to move your foot? I'm afraid you are standing on my toes.' If you are so inconsiderate as to block somebody's path or view, they'll say 'Excuse me'.

The British apologise all the time, for everything, especially for matters which are not their fault. If you bump into someone in the street because you were careless and concentrating on the shop windows, they'll say 'Sorry'.

If you visit someone, they'll say: 'I'm so sorry about the weather. Sorry you got wet.' And later 'I'm so sorry I can't offer you anything special for dinner. I'm so sorry I'm not a good cook' (especially if the hostess is renowned for her cookery skills and the meal is elaborate).

MAKING THE RIGHT NOISES

Good manners demand that the British always say the right thing. The right thing is not necessarily the truth. It is what the other person wants to hear. This is called 'making the right noises'.

If a British woman is given a sweater for her birthday and in a colour she hates, she'll claim that this is a lovely colour, that she has always wanted a sweater like this. The next day she'll take it back to the shop and exchange it for something else.

The British will applaud a speaker who has just given a talk at the local horticultural society, and even seek him out afterwards to tell him how much they have enjoyed his talk. As soon as he has left the hall, they'll remark to their seat neighbour: 'This evening was a waste of time. The speaker doesn't have a clue about what grows well on our local soil.'

Hospitality

Take compliments, praise and any gestures of approval with a pinch of salt. They may or may not be meant like this. This applies to invitations, too. If you meet someone for the first time, they may be generous with invitations. 'Of course you must come and stay with us if you ever come to Scotland' or 'No need to pay for a bedsit. You can stay with us, we have a spare room' or 'We have a holiday home on the south coast. It's all yours.'

Don't take up an invitation unless you are 100 per cent sure that they mean it. Say something polite and non-committal, such as 'Yes, maybe, that would be nice, thanks' and talk about a different subject. If they mean it, they will repeat the invitation on another occasion.

If you accept hospitality for more than two nights, always offer to pay. Your hosts will refuse to accept payment, but you must repeat your offer. Pay attention to how they refuse.

If they say 'You don't *have* to pay' it means they would like you to. Handle the matter tactfully, for example by leaving a thank-you card and a cheque in your room.

If they say, on the other hand 'Don't be ridiculous, you don't have to pay. We couldn't possibly take money from you', then you buy a bottle of wine or a bunch of flowers, or take your hosts out for a meal. Leave a thank-you note without cheque.

If you come from a country where it is the custom to be generous to guests, and nobody would dream of accepting money for having someone stay for a few days, the attitude of some British people to hospitality can come as a shock. It may be because of their own financial situation.

Never say never

The British avoid saying 'no' for fear of disappointing, hurting or offending you. For example, a group of friends discuss hiring a minibus to travel to London to see a musical. You offer to organise it. You make enquiries, find out how much the cost per person will be. 'Will you come if I organise it for 2 December, and bring the money on the day?' you ask. They will all say yes, and then nobody will turn up. Some won't even bother to phone and say that they have changed their mind. You will go to London on your own and pay the huge bill for the theatre tickets and the bus hire.

If you confront your friends afterwards, they will murmur something about 'had relatives to stay', 'had to work late that evening', 'couldn't make it', and comfort you 'maybe I'll come another day when you're doing something like that again'.

A secure method of nailing them down is to ask for advance payment before you book, organise, or order anything for them. If they are truly interested, they won't mind. If they act offended, they never meant to pay anyway.

UNDERSTANDING THE ANIMAL RIGHTS MOVEMENT

If Britons observe cruelty to humans, they may get upset. But if they see an animal treated cruelly they are outraged and take immediate action.

Don't wear a fur coat in Britain. You would be challenged in the streets and accused of cruelty.

Some radical animal rights groups don't hesitate to harm humans in order to protect animals. Violence and cruelty against humans gives them the media coverage they need to draw attention to the suffering of animals, for example of calves being shipped abroad under cruel conditions.

Most British people don't agree that the cause justifies the means. But tread carefully in case you are talking to someone who feels strongly about the subject, for or against animal rights.

'YOU OLD BASTARD'

Everyone knows that the British don't possess a sense of humour, except the British.

Well, they do, but the things which make Britons chuckle take a while to get used to. (I found it easier to joke with people in northeast China than with Britons. Is it possible that the German and the Chinese sense of humour is more related than the German and the British, despite common Anglo-Saxon roots?)

The good news is that British jokes are rarely cruel. They are just silly, and occasionally even funny. They like to joke about other nations, and the tales usually involve Germans ('krauts') getting up early in the morning to place towels on deckchairs, and French people ('frogs') eating everything as long as it is well-cooked.

Here is a typical example of the funnier kind:

Q: What is paradise?
A: A world in which the police are British, the mechanics are Germans, the cooks are French and the lovers are Italian.

Q: And what is hell?
A: A world in which the police are Italians, the mechanics are French, the cooks are British and the lovers are German. (Got it?)

An expression of humour you may encounter is calling one's best friend 'you old bastard' or 'silly old cow'. Don't be shocked. These are often meant as terms of endearment and won't result in a fist fight. But it is important to get the tone right, and foreigners rarely succeed. It might be wise not to call your boss a stupid asshole.

WEARING THE RIGHT CLOTHES

One of the nice things about Britain is that you can wear whatever you like. You can walk down the high street or sit in the underground train wearing the weirdest clothes, and nobody will take any notice. They won't chuckle behind your back or point fingers at you.

The British are used to seeing foreign nationals in their national costumes. Even at work you can wear whatever is appropriate in your culture. London Underground staff from Asian origins often wear navy blue turbans matching their navy blue uniform, and female Muslim bank cashiers wear headscarves.

The British must be the most tolerant of all nations as far as clothing is concerned.

Here are some rules to follow, although they are not strict: If you work in an office, wear a **suit**. Women can wear very short skirts at work showing a lot of leg, but the shoulders must remain covered, and cleavage is taboo. Men must wear long trousers at work.

For **casual wear** in summer, men or women can wear shorts, sandals, and sleeveless tops. In the home, many people like wearing tracksuit bottoms instead of trousers. White trainers are popular as casual footwear, especially among young people. In the evening, women can expose their shoulders and show cleavage if they wish, but men should wear long sleeves.

Navy blue and grey are colours which are always right in an office for women and men. The equivalent for **evening functions** is black.

Men should not wear skirts or gowns except as part of a national or regional costume, like the Scottish kilt.

In the countryside, people tend to wear old, baggy, comfortable clothes, often in tweeds or in muted colours.

QUEUING

There's just one aspect of British life which is reflected correctly in English language textbooks abroad. The British **do** queue. There are queues in front of ticket counters at railway stations, at bus stops even when there is no bus in sight, in banks, post offices and shops.

I was once in a railway station when police announced that there was a bomb alert, and would everyone please leave the building as soon as possible? Nobody panicked, nobody ran to the exit, nobody pushed others aside to get out first. The several hundred people formed three well-behaved queues at the three exits, and left the bomb-threatened station in an orderly manner.

Never jump a queue, however much you are in a hurry. Some understanding supermarket managers have introduced extra cash-tills for 'baskets with fewer than five items' which you can use if you are in a hurry (and have fewer than five items in your basket).

A special queuing system operates for multiple counters, *eg* at large post offices. There is a single queue, running zigzag across a large hall, leading to not one but a dozen or more counters. As soon as any of the counters is free, the person at the front of the queue goes there. This avoids the frustration of always being in the queue behind people with complicated time-consuming requests.

If you are at the front of such a queue, sometimes it's difficult to see which counter becomes available when. Optical and acoustic signals help: flashing lights, and recorded voices 'Please proceed to counter 17. Counter 17 is ready to serve you.'

CASE STUDIES

Beat walks through the snow

'One evening, the weather forecast said heavy snow overnight. So I got up an hour earlier than usual in the morning, put on my boots and warm clothes, and made my way slowly through the high snow. In Switzerland, snow like this is normal for several weeks in winter. But when I arrived, I found I was the only one who had turned up for work! I started working anyway, and finally some of my colleagues arrived. They said it had taken them four hours to get there. This was ridiculous, their journey wasn't further than mine. All they had to do was get up a bit earlier. To my surprise, they just worked for half an hour, then left again. They said they had to leave now because it would take them so long to get home.

'Later I found out that it was the company's policy to pay staff in case of severe weather for the full day's work even if they arrived late or left early – provided they turned up at all.

'There was an hourly broadcast of bread baking recipes and other survival tips, as if this was a real emergency. It was a great pretence.'

Laurenz learns to like the English way

'When I first arrived, I was lonely and unhappy. This was partly because the British are reserved and it was difficult to make friends, but part of it was in my mind. I expected the English to be really cold and reserved – that's what the French think about them. So I didn't really try to make friends. I was not talking to people, because I couldn't speak the language well, partly because of my prejudices. After a year everything changed completely: I met Richard, my future husband. He was the first person who was really interested in me. I met his friends. Now I like the English people and the way they live. They are brilliant, caring and relaxed. I wouldn't think of going back to France.

'The weather really did bother me. I expected the worst. But it's similar to Paris, perhaps it rains a little more.

'I did not meet any prejudice when I was working as an au pair, and later as a waitress, as an assistant in a nursing home, as an advertising sales rep. But now I'm working as a bank cashier, there are two or three of the bank customers who resent it. I speak English fluently by now, but they make a point of not 'understanding' my accent. Deep down they think that banking is an upper class job, which should be reserved for upper class English people. The same type of person doesn't object to a foreign waitress!

'Some British people like to remind you all the time that you are a foreigner, and try to make you feel like an outsider. Don't let them do this to you. There are not many of them, but as a foreigner you must be strong if you want to take your place in the community.'

Deborah is surprised by the weather

'My first surprise when I came to Britain was the weather. In America, we imagine that British weather is dull and rainy all the time. But there is at least some sun every day.

'What I admire about the British yet find difficult to cope with is the subtlety. They are masters in the art of subtlety. It's amazing how much can be said with how few words. You have to listen carefully to get the full and true meaning. This can lead to misunderstandings. People think you've got the message when you haven't.'

Monica notices the freedom and prejudice

'The biggest difference between Britain and Korea is that people in Britain have so much more individual freedom. I noticed that the police here don't control people's lives and interfere so much. On the other hand, I was reassured when they were there when I needed them. There was a nasty incident when the landlord in a bed and breakfast place tried to climb into my bed at night! I fled and told neighbours, who called the police. The police asked me if I wanted the man prosecuted, but I was afraid because I was new to the country, uncertain about the legal situation, and I didn't want to stir up trouble. I just asked them to give the man a stern warning, which they did. Now I am more confident, and if a similar situation arose I would want them to take action against the offender.

'Most people in Britain are not racist, or try not to be. But I've also had nasty experiences, with people shouting at me "F*** off, go home to your country." They would even say aloud "How can a nice English boy be married to that kind of woman?" (meaning to a Korean woman). I no longer take notice of such comments, but they were upsetting at first.'

Francesca observes the 'right noises'

'I was living in a flatshare with two other Italian students and an English girl. The English girl had a visitor for tea. This young man admired her very much and brought her a Christmas present. It was a lovely basket with fragrant soap, foam bath and body lotion. I was really envious, and so were the other two. We thought she was lucky that a young man spoilt her that much. She seemed to appreciate the gift: she kept telling the young man that this was just what she wanted, that she would take a bubble bath that night, that she found the fragrances delightful.

'As soon as he had left, she dumped the cosmetics in a corner. "Why can't men be more imaginative? I'll never use it. I still have exactly the same stuff from last Christmas. I bet he will give me body lotion and soap again next year."

'I was shocked. I felt sorry for the young man. I felt like running after him and asking him to give the soap to me instead! It's one thing being polite, and another telling lies.

'I spent Christmas day with a friend's family. "I'll have to hang up those awful bird plates because Aunt Jean is coming," the hostess sighed. "You see, she gave me one of these collector's plates with a bird motif for Christmas five years ago. I must have made the right noises, saying how lovely they are, for she has been giving me one of them each year. I just hate them, but of course I have to display them whenever she comes."

'I asked why she didn't tell her aunt that she didn't want any more bird plates. "It's simply not done. You must make the right noises."

'I was there when the aunt arrived and handed over her present. I was so ashamed listening to the hostess praising the lovely bird plate and claiming that she looked forward to expanding the collection.'

Markus leads a German invasion

'I found the British friendly and open-minded, and met no prejudice – until I got together with a few German friends. We were just a handful of students having fun, without doing anything offensive at all. But the British people on the bus looked at us with expressions which ranged from hostility to fear, some even moved away from us. They behaved as if there was a German enemy invasion.'

Lynne dislikes the gossip

'I'm still puzzled by what people here are and aren't willing to speak up about. Brits make a fuss about things Americans wouldn't even notice, and there are things which the Brits ignore but the American would shout about. Culturally, this is something that still trips me up occasionally.

'People here are very rarely direct in their dealings with each other. If someone here has a problem with someone else, they will seldom take it up with that person directly. Instead they will talk about it with various third parties, to vent their feelings. Often the complaint will find its way back to the original target via the rumour mill. That person can then choose to act on it by changing his/her behaviour, or ignoring it, or retaliating by saying other things to those third paries.

'I find it perilously close to what American consider to be sniping and backbiting, even though that's not the way Brits see it. If I have a problem with what someone is doing, I tell them directly. Most Brits consider that blunt to the point of rudeness; it's just not the done thing.

'I like the Scottish attitude towards balancing work and life. People here are not expected to make school or their jobs the entire focus of their lives. People get a decent amount of holidays, and are expected to want to spend time with their families.'

Fiona is puzzled by the class system
'In Australia, everyone is treated as equals and we get along with everyone, but to many British people it is important what someone's last name is, who their grandfather is, and where they went to school.'

Carina learns to allow private space
'One of the challenges during my first five years was adapting to the different social codes. The differences between Sweden and Britain are subtle, not immediately obvious, but profound. I found I had to allow for more personal space in communicating with people, particularly in London, and not to get too familiar, too soon. After a while, I grew to love the 'extra personal space' I had problems with initially; I found it suited me well.

'I found it unsettling that my sense of humour was not intelligible to the 'natives'. When I joked, I got blank faces in response. I could appreciate jokes coming from the British people, but Swedish humour translated badly. That took some time getting used to.

'What baffled me was that people made verbal commitments to all sorts of things, and didn't try to carry them through. They promised on the phone to get back to me, or to do this or that, and nothing happened.'

4

Learning the Language

The better you can understand, speak and write English, the easier you will find life in the UK. For most jobs you need at least basic English; for others you must be fluent in the language. Even if you don't plan to work in the UK, you'll need language skills for your daily life: shopping, talking to neighbours, watching television, making phone calls.

If you don't plan to leave immediately, enrol for an evening class in English, or buy a complete course. Courses which combine books with audio tapes are usually the best.

Many foreigners who learnt English at school or college and who can write and read fluently find it difficult to understand spoken English or to speak English.

You will also observe that everyday English as it is spoken in the UK is different to the English you learnt at school.

UNDERSTANDING ACCENTS

'But you speak English better than we do!' is a comment you will hear all the time. This is because the British people judge the quality of spoken English by the correctness of the grammar.

If you have learnt all the grammar rules and apply them, your English is considered wonderful, even if your pronunciation leaves something to be desired.

There are so many different regional accents (Scottish, Welsh, northern, southern *etc*), not to speak of national accents (American, Australian *etc*), that the British feel it is impossible to judge whether the pronunciation is good.

The use of **correct grammar**, as taught at schools and colleges abroad, indicates middle or upper class. Working-class people use a different grammar.

Some people (especially middle-class parents) are very particular about the use of correct grammar. Here is a typical conversation between a middle-class mother and her ten-year-old daughter, which I overheard:

'Mum, I've made a new friend. Jennie is sitting next to me at school. I want her to come to my birthday party.'

'Hm. Does she speak nicely?'

'Yes, Mum. The teacher says she speaks like Princess Diana.'

'Oh, she sounds like a nice sort of girl. Of course you may invite her to your birthday party. I'm glad you have found such a nice friend.'

Try to keep your supposedly 'upper-class' grammar as it will help you in your career. This is easier said than done, because if you are living and working in a working class environment you automatically imitate their phrases ('That ain't no good').

As mentioned before, **pronunciation** is more a matter of regional accents than of class. There is one exception: working class people often drop the 'h' at the beginning of a word: ' 'arry! I 'aven't got any 'ot water for the coffee!'

'Good' English is also measured by the use of swear-words. The fewer you use, the better is your English. A sentence which contains swear-words is not good English even if you pronounce it correctly and present it in perfect grammar.

The British public debate eagerly whether swear-words have a place in radio and television: should the broadcasts reflect the language of the people, or should they set an example of 'good' English?

'Wrong English'

The British like plays on words, and deliberately mis-spell words to attract attention, for example in business names such as Nu Doors (new doors) or Kall Kwik (call quick), or in magazine headlines.

LEARNING ENGLISH FROM BOOKS AND NEWSPAPERS

If there is an **international bookshop** in your home country, buy some English-language books. Read a few paragraphs before you buy a book: if you understand most of it, but some words are new, than it's ideal. If you understand only a few words per page, it's too difficult. For people whose English vocabulary is limited, illustrated non-fiction books about their hobbies or work are best: you can guess from the pictures what the captions mean.

Many **libraries**, especially university libraries, have English books. Sometimes the English shelf of a library consists of nothing but literary classics (such as Charles Dickens) and Agatha Christie's crime novels. The classics will certainly widen your vocabulary, even if they don't supply up-to-date phrases. Agatha Christie's books are highly suitable: they are written in clear, precise English with simple words and short sentences, and are therefore easy to read.

I and several of my friends found that the best books for learning modern English are the **romantic novels** published by Mills & Boon. The plots are predictable (the heroine will get her tall dark handsome man in chapter 10). But the books are written in excellent style, using straightforward, clear, everyday language. They are easy to understand but use a wider vocabulary than Agatha Christie.

In Britain you can buy these paperback novels from bookshops and newsagents. They are not expensive, but if money is tight, you can get them for a few pence from charity shops or boot fairs.

If you are still abroad, it may be difficult to get hold of them. Mills & Boon offer an annual subscription, but you have to buy twelve paperbacks each month for a year. This may be right for you if you are an avid reader and if you enjoy romances.

Read British **newspapers** and **magazines**. You may be able to buy them at railway stations or airports in your home country. You can also take out a subscription to a magazine. Choose a general interest magazine, or one about your hobbies or area of work.

British daily newspapers are divided in two groups, 'broadsheets' and 'tabloids'. Broadsheet papers such *The Times*, *The Guardian* and *The Independent* are so large in size that it's awkward to read them while commuting on the bus or the underground. They usually provide more balanced views and more background information than the tabloids, but are also more difficult to read.

If your English is not very good yet, it is best to stick to the tabloids such as *The Sun* which are written in short sentences and simple words. If you have studied English for several years and find most tabloids too sensational in their approach, but the broadsheets are still too difficult, try the *Daily Mail*. This is probably the most upmarket of the tabloids, and many foreign nationals find it relatively easy to read. At a similar level is *The Evening Standard*, but this is sold only in the London area.

Is writing well important in your area of work, for example, if you want to work as a secretary or in public relations? Then put aside 15 minutes every day to copy an article from a newspaper or magazine or a couple of pages from a novel.

STUDYING ENGLISH IN THE UK

Language tourism is an important industry in Britain. Many foreign students and business people come to Britain for a few weeks to study English. In some areas, especially along the coast in the southeast, the economy depends on language students. This means that a wide choice of courses is available.

You can, for example:

- Come to the UK for several months just to study the language in a full time course.

- Attend a course for a couple of weeks or more to brush up your language skills before taking up a job.

- Enrol for a course in English for Special Purposes which will help you gain the vocabulary for your skills area.

- Study English while you go job-hunting.

- Take a language course which includes work experience in a British company to prove that you are able to work in a British environment.

- Work during daytime and attend an evening class once a week to improve your language skills.

- Work as an au pair and attend a language college once a day.

You can book language courses in Britain while you are still in your home country, either through a travel agency or by contacting language schools directly. You can get addresses of language schools from the British Tourist Office in your home country (and see Useful Addresses).

The UKCOSA has published a leaflet *Learning English in the UK* (see Useful Addresses).

Checklist: Choosing a full-time course

- Is the school or college accredited by the British Council?

- How many hours tuition each week?

- How many students are there in each class?

- Do they come from different countries (if all students are Italian, they will probably talk Italian instead of English)?

- How long does the course last?
- How much does the course cost?
- Can I afford it?
- Will the course cover my specific needs (for example, business English)?
- Can I combine the course with learning other skills?
- Does the course lead to a recognised qualification?
- Will the school arrange accommodation? (Type? Cost? Will there be other students in the same house? If yes, which nationalities?)
- If I plan to take up a job after completing the course: is the school in the same area as the company?
- If I haven't found a job yet: is the school in an area where I'm likely to find employment?

GAINING A QUALIFICATION

If you want a qualification which is recognised worldwide, choose a course which prepares you for the Cambridge examinations. There are several levels. The two best-known are:

- First
- Proficiency.

You don't have to go to Cambridge to do these exams. You can do them in about 1,000 centres worldwide. The exams take place simultaneously in June and December in every centre, using the same exam papers.

Your language school will arrange for you to attend the exam at the nearest centre. Of course, if you have your First or Proficiency in your pocket before you apply for a job or before you go to Britain, you will find it easier to get employment or be accepted on a course of study.

You can apply to sit the examinations without attending a course first, but remember that the standards are high and that particular attention is paid to understanding and speaking. If you are good at reading, writing, grammar and spelling, you may still fail if you can't speak or understand well.

The First Certificate

The First Certificate is suitable for people who have studied English for about six years at school before they take the course. The course lasts about twelve weeks full-time, or one year in evening classes. It is a recognised qualification for everyone who needs to be fluent in written and spoken English for work purposes.

The Certificate of Proficiency

The Certificate of Proficiency aims at a high level of understanding and fluency. If you have studied English at school and college for about nine years, this course is for you. In some countries, this certificate is regarded as a step towards an English degree or a translator's diploma. The certificate also confirms that you have mastered the English language well enough to teach it in your home country.

If you plan to study at university in Britain, you may be required to sit for the Certificate of Proficiency examination to make sure you can follow the lectures and write the required essays.

The examination consists of five papers:

1. **Reading comprehension**. Candidates are tested on vocabulary, grammar, comprehension, and understanding the contents of a text.

2. **Composition**. Candidates must write two compositions or essays. They are given several topics to choose from.

3. **Use of English**. This tests again the candidate's ability to understand a text and to summarise it, and there are grammar exercises.

4. **Listening comprehension**. This section is often perceived as the most difficult. Candidates listen to a tape of authentic English in different realistic situations, for example, against the background noises of an airport, or speaking in regional accents. They have to answer questions to prove their understanding.

5. **Interview**. Candidates are given photographs or short texts to discuss, or problem solving tasks. The interviewer and the candidate talk for 15 minutes, usually on a one-to-one basis.

If you pass the exam, you will be awarded a certificate in grade A,B or C. D, E and U are fail grades.

For further information, contact: Marketing Division, University of Cambridge, Local Examinations Syndicate, 1 Hills Road, Cambridge CB1 2EU. Tel: (01223) 553311, Fax: (01223) 460278. e-mail: *efl@ucles.org.uk*

LEARNING ENGLISH FOR SPECIAL PURPOSES

If you want to learn English mostly for work, then try to find a course which concentrates on a specific subject. There are many English courses on specialist subjects, but you may have to shop around and contact many language schools until you find the right one. Tell the schools what you want or need: they may be able to meet your requirements.

Sometimes they arrange guided tours to businesses and companies (banks, factories *etc*) for students who share the same professional interests. If you take one-to-one tuition, it is often possible for you and your tutor to visit a shop or business in your specific type of work.

Evendine Colleges in London offer several specialist courses on an individual or group basis, including English for the Legal Profession, English for the Medical Profession, English for Banking and Finance. A course in Medical English is also available from the Edinburgh School of English. EF offer specialist courses, such as English for Law and English for Telecommunications during specific weeks only.

English for Academic Purposes
A four-week course with 28 lessons per week run by St Giles Colleges in Brighton and London prepares students for study at a British university. They can help in preparing for university entrance exams. Students need at least intermediate level English for this course.

English for Art & Design
St London Highgate has a course especially for people working or studying in this field. The morning lessons cover general English, while the afternoons focus on topics such as interior design, photography, fashion and art history.

English for Lawyers

The London School of English offers a range of intensive English language programmes for commercial lawyers, public sector lawyers, criminal lawyers and public prosecutors, as well as courses aimed specifically at lawyers under the age of 25. Anglo Continental also has courses in English for the legal practice.

Teaching training

If you are, or want to become, a teacher of English, contact the major English language schools. Many are offering teacher training courses as well as specialist language training for already qualified teachers. See also page 67.

Business English

Business English courses are available both in the UK and in other countries. Most of the larger language schools in Britain offer specialist business courses. These courses are useful for secretaries, managers and marketing people. Try to find one which teaches spoken as well as written business English. For these courses, you will normally need at least intermediate level English.

The Edinburgh School of English, based in Scotland, runs a course called Executive Essential English. This runs for two or more weeks and includes 28 group lessons per week, which cover the use of English for negotiations, presentations and meetings; business communications such as business letters, using the telephone, making appointments; English in business situations such as receiving clients and showing visitors around. In addition, the course offers eight individual lessons per week, where the student and the tutor concentrate on particular areas of interest, such as tourism, banking or marketing. The school can arrange accommodation with host families

St Giles Colleges in Brighton and Central London offer English for Executives courses which use simulated business situations and role-play to develop your presentation and negotiation skills. You can choose to study 20, 30 or 35 lessons weekly. A more general English for Business course, full-day over four, eight or twelve weeks, take places in London, Eastbourne and Brighton.

Regent Language Training, Pilgrims, Bell, and Eastbourne School of English also have courses in Business English. The London School of English has courses aimed at secretaries and personal assistants.

Some business English courses can lead to examinations by the London Chamber of Commerce and Industry.

English for Tourism

English for Tourism courses are rarer. But if you are working, or planning to work, in catering, you can choose a course in Holiday English instead. Your fellow students will study for a different purpose, but you will still learn all the vocabulary and phrases of the hotel and restaurant trade.

St Giles Colleges in Brighton and London offer four-week full-day English for Tourism classes which comprise general English lessons in the morning and cover tourism-related topics in the afternoon, such as travel agents, reservations, cancellations, hotels and restaurants. You need intermediate level English to participate in this course.

The Edinburgh School of English has an English for Tourism course which includes visits to tourist attractions in Edinburgh. Evendine Colleges have individual and group courses not only in English for the Travel and Tourism Industry, but also English for Airline Staff and Cabin Crew.

Other organisations offering English for tourism courses are Regent and Anglo Continental.

English for selling and presentations

This is a practical course specially designed for anyone who needs to make business presentations in English – for example, managers, secretaries, public relations and sales people. You will make several presentations which are recorded on video so that you can watch, analyse and improve your performance. In the mornings you get group tuition in grammar and conversation. In the afternoons you practise the specific language you need in your profession.

This course is offered by the Cicero language school and costs currently £508 per week including accommodation, or £423 per week without accommodation.

English plus work experience

Some language schools offer language courses combined with (unpaid) work experience in your chosen field. This will not only help you use your language skills in a practical context, but will also boost your CV if you plan to apply for a job in the UK.

Schools which arrange work experiences include St Giles Colleges in London, Brighton and Eastbourne, and HF International Language Schools which can offer language courses combined with internships in sales, finance, education and other fields, and The London School of English. Regent offers a combination of business

English courses with four-week work experience placements in a variety of business sectors (excluding banking, finance or law). Bell offers a combination of two or more weeks language study at intermediate or advanced level and a work placement of one month or more, but this is available only for EU passport holders.

COMBINING LANGUAGE LEARNING WITH OTHER SKILLS

Some of the bigger language schools in the UK offer courses which combine languages with the learning of a **practical skill**. You learn English in the morning, and study a different subject in the afternoon. This gives you the chance to practise your English in a realistic environment, and it breaks up the concentrated language study which can be tiring.

Practical skills offered by UK language schools include drama, horse riding, golf, tennis, local history, health and fitness.

Some of these courses relate to a particular trade or industry, and although they aim at hobbyists they can help you learn and use the vocabulary of your trade.

If you are already qualified or experienced in the beauty industry, you will learn the English terms and phrases, and possibly pick up new skills as well, such as reflexology.

A combined English and cookery course can be useful if you plan to find work in domestic employment. This course is also organised by Cicero, and you can choose different levels, depending on how much English and cookery you already know.

Price example: English and aromatherapy, including accommodation, £480 per week.

LIVING WITH THE TEACHER

If you want to immerse yourself in the culture and language for a while before you start job-hunting, working or studying at university, consider a home language programme. The student lives in the teacher's home and has lessons there.

Naturally, the success of this scheme depends on how well matched the student and the teacher are. Spending all your time with a person you dislike can be a big problem, especially if you've booked several weeks. It is important that you tell the agency or organiser what your needs are – so that they can allocate the right teacher to you. If you need maximum privacy where nobody enters your room in your absence, want to smoke in the bedroom, require a private bathroom, or if you specifically want a teacher who shares your passion for rock music and rabbits, or is knowledgeable about stock market matters, ask.

Norman Renshaw of InTuition believes that the one-to-one tuition is ideal for business and professional people who want to learn language skills relevant for their work. 'The teachers have been chosen for their expertise in teaching English for specific purposes, and many of them have had other professions before becoming teachers.' At the moment, InTuition offers specialist tuition in the fields of aviation industry, banking and finance, computing, electronics, engineering, marketing, pharmaceuticals, electronics and the law. If you intend to work in a specific sector and need the language skills for it, it is worth asking if the organisation can find a suitable teacher for you.

John Hall of Concorde International says that they depend on the student to supply the information which helps them select the most suitable family, and that a representative will contact all students within two days of arrival to check that everything is as it should be. 'If the students are not happy, for any reason at all, we will offer another family immediately.'

Staying in the teacher's home is also a good option if you plan to stay and study with your spouse, partner or friend who has a similar level of English skills. The minimum stay is normally one week, but the course can be booked for several weeks or months.

CHOOSING COURSES FOR CHILDREN

Children can often pick up a language much quicker than adults, especially if they live in the country. However, if they don't speak English on their arrival, it may set them back in their school education.

Some language schools offer special courses for juniors. Choose one which groups children of similar ages. Children's attention time is limited, so the ideal course provides plenty of activities.

ATTENDING EVENING AND PART-TIME CLASSES

Evening and part-time classes in English are run by language schools and adult education centres. Find a job and/or accommodation first, then look around for a local course at a suitable level.

Daytime classes (for example, one day per week, or two hours on three days of the week) are often attended by au pairs. If you stay for at least one year, you may be able to finish your course with one of the Cambridge certificate exams.

A three-term (one year) course on Thursday evenings at the Tunbridge Wells adult education centre, leading to the Proficiency exam, costs about £290 plus examination fee. Many adult centres offer beginners classes in Welsh.

Free lessons

Some adult education centres run one-year courses, two hours each week, which provide an introduction to English grammar and an opportunity to practise spoken English. The larger of these centres organise them at two levels (beginners and moving-on). If your English is good already, you may feel out of place even in the moving-on group.

If you are a resident in Britain you can attend these courses free of charge. Most of these courses take place during daytime.

HAVING PRIVATE LESSONS

The quickest way of learning English is of course one-to-one tuition. The tutor can focus on your individual requirements. Most language schools provide this service, but it is expensive.

A cheaper way of getting one-to-one tuition is to arrange an exchange deal: one lesson each week in English in return for one lesson each week in your native tongue. Don't expect too great teaching skills from a friendly person who is not a qualified teacher. However, these exchange lessons work well for conversation skills.

CHECKLIST

- Have I looked at ways of improving my English before going to the UK?

- Do I have the time to enrol for a course in my home country?

- Where can I buy or borrow English-language books?

- Have I subscribed to an English-language magazine or newspaper?

- Have I sent for brochures of language schools?

- Are there any language schools in the area where I want to live?
- If I am already in the UK: would I benefit from a course? Have I obtained the local adult education brochure?
- Which schools offer courses suitable for my ability and my interests?
- Which courses would help me in my career?
- Can I afford to spend the money and the time?

CASE STUDIES

Laurenz learns by listening

'One of my reasons for going to England rather than to Germany was that I had learnt a little more English at school in Paris than German. I attended a course for a while, but what really helped me improve my English was working as a waitress for nine months. I can't say I enjoyed the job, but I liked meeting people. The constant contact with so many people helped improve my spoken English no end.'

Sabine's employer pays for the course

'I had studied English at school in Germany until I was 17, but my language skills were far from perfect. It was a bit embarrassing for a bilingual secretary. So I booked for a one-year evening class to gain the Cambridge First Certificate. One day I took courage and asked my employers if they would pay for the course. I expected them to refuse, but they agreed immediately.'

Antonio gets a surprise

'I had studied English in Italy and I thought that, with the help of the dictionary which I had used throughout college and university, I was quite fluent. It turned out that many of the words in the dictionary were inappropriate. I used some phrases in my CV and the recruitment consultant asked: "What do you mean by that? Is that an Italian word? Why don't you translate it into English?" An elderly neighbour commented: "How quaint. We used to say that in my youth."

'On the other hand, there are many words which the British use every day, which are not included in a dictionary. Each day I chose one of these, wrote it on a slip of paper and stuck it on my computer screen. I remember that the list included 'nitty-gritty, to fancy something, to be after someone, in-house, state-of-the-art, spanky bollocks.' The last was used a lot in the office but nobody would tell me what it meant. They laughed when they saw it pinned up on my screen. I think I can guess the appropriate meaning now but I would not recommend using it.

'After six months, I bought a different dictionary and binned the old one.'

Martin learns to speak English

'At school in Japan, I always got the top grades in English. This is why my friends called me by an English name. I was good at grammar and spelling, but like most of my classmates I did not want to speak English. I was afraid of making mistakes. My teacher tried to make us speak but without success. Within three weeks of being in England, it suddenly clicked. I had to speak if I wanted to survive. I was no longer afraid. I realised that mistakes didn't matter at all. What counted was that I could make myself understood.'

Lynne struggles with the local slang

'Although I'm American and English is my native language, the slang puzzled me. Even when I could understand the words, I couldn't understand the meaning. The local usage varies widely. Most people know about 'rubbers' (which can be erasers or condoms). 'Suspenders' are not what holds up the trousers of a fat man, they are what holds up stocking on a lady, what American would call a 'garter belt'. 'Braces' are not on the teeth, they are the things which hold up the trousers on fat men. Oh yes, and jeans are 'trousers' not 'pants' since 'pants' under underpants. A 'vest' is an undershirt, and what Americans call 'vests' are 'waistcoats' in Britain.

'Being 'chuffed' is pleased, and 'pissed' means drunk.

'Here in Aberdeen in Scotland, there are some even less predictable words like 'messages' being groceries.

'Oh my god was it difficult to understand the local accents! For a while I was not convinced that people spoke English at all. I remember sitting in a bus behind two old biddies who were chatting away, and I was wondering if maybe they were speaking Norwegian. Now I have no difficulty with it, in fact it sounds normal to me and an American accent sounds quite hard, but it took me over two years to get to that point.

'There are a lot of local accents packed into very small areas, and getting comfortable with one is no guarantee you'll understand the rest. Each part of Aberdeen has its own accent. For example, the Queen's Road area in the west has a dead posh accent, and Torry in the south, now that's an accent you can spot miles away. My husband assures me it used to be possible to identify which street people lived on by their accent. Of course these days the accents are smoothed out somewhat because of increased mobility.

'I noticed that the further north on the mainland you get, the more impenetrable the accent is. I find the Highland and Island accents lovely, but a Peterhead accent (northeast corner of Scotland) is completely impossible to understand, even for other Scots.'

Fiona struggles with the Scottish accent
'When I first arrived in Scotland I really struggled with the accents. But by the time I left Scotland to live in London I could understand every single word. I have never had trouble with the English in London.'

Sigal speaks and adopts the accent
'As an Australian, I found the London accent easy to understand. My accent has become more British than Australian.'

POINTS TO CONSIDER

1. Assess your language skills critically. Which are your weaknesses? Do you need a wider vocabulary, do you need to learn the specialist vocabulary of your trade? Are you struggling with grammar or pronunciation? Do you find it difficult to speak?

2. Look at different ways of improving your English before you go to Britain. Consider the time and money available. Which options mentioned in this chapter are realistic? Do you have any other ideas?

3. Would a course in English for special purposes help you find a job or make your daily life easier? If yes, which types of courses would be suitable?

4. Would it be better to take a course while you are still in your home country, or to take a course in the UK? Consider all the factors, including time and money.

5

Finding Work

The employment situation in Britain currently is good. Sometimes a big company closes and cause temporary local unemployment, or a major industry sector is in difficulty which affects jobs, but most people who want to work will find work.

Your chances of finding a job depend on your skills, and the type of work you want to do.

Your job prospects are excellent if you are aiming for one of the following sectors:

- nursing and caring
- domestic
- teaching (especially technology or IT skills)
- engineering
- building and construction.

FINDING NURSING AND CARING WORK

Most British hospitals complain that they do not have enough nurses; their staff often leave as soon as they finish their training to take on better paid work in the private sector or abroad. If you have a nursing qualification, you will find a job easily. Apply directly to the hospitals in the area. Alternatively, register with a specialist agency. You may have to prove that your qualification is the equivalent of a British nursing qualification, and possibly undergo some assessment or additional training. If you are looking for a first job, you can choose nursing as a career. Hospitals usually provide accommodation for their student nurses, and with a British nursing qualification, you'll never be out of a job.

Residential care homes for the elderly or disabled people are always looking for staff, with our without qualifications. Unlike hospitals which require specific qualifications, residential care homes appreciate any kind of care-related certificate. They will gladly take you on even if you have no caring qualifications or experience whatsoever, as long as you have a mature attitude and show a sincere interest in caring. If you want to make caring your career, ask if they will sponsor you for qualifications. You can gain basic qualifications in care work (usually on the NVQ – National Vocational Qualification) scheme, and once you have qualifications, you will earn more. If you need to earn more money quickly, consider taking a night care job. Most nursing homes are desperate for night care staff and are willing to pay accordingly.

Full-time and part-time jobs are advertised in the local newspapers. Once you have care home experience and basic qualifications, you may prefer to register with an agency and do private care work for individual patients in their home.

FINDING TEACHING WORK

The shortage of teachers is so alarming that the UK government runs a campaign to entice more people into this career.

If you are a qualified teacher, you should find it easy to get a job, but bear in mind that most teachers are recruited for an academic year, which starts in September. If you arrive in the middle of the year, few jobs will be available. In this case, register with a supply teachers agency. They can help you get temporary teaching work, standing in for teachers who are ill.

If teaching appeals to you, but you have no qualification, apply for a job as a classroom assistant or assistant teacher. You will not have the same responsibility, and you won't earn as much as a 'real' teacher, but it can be the ideal entry into the career. Many schools are glad to recruit native speakers as assistants for the foreign language department. If you want to gain a teaching qualification quickly, consider the City & Guilds courses. There are run part-time by many adult education centres and qualify you to teach adults and over-16s.

You can also teach part-time at adult education centres, in evening classes or Saturday workshops. Most adult education centres will consider new teachers who can offer languages or unusual skills. You don't need to be a qualified teacher for an adult education centre, but most centres will encourage you to study for a basic teaching qualification. They may even pay the course fee for you. Adult education teachers earn around £15 per hour, but you are expected to do a lot of paperwork unpaid, and the colleges reserve the right to cancel your courses at short notice – although they expect you to commit yourself up to two years in advance.

FINDING DOMESTIC WORK

Cleaner

Cleaners are always in demand. Your employers are people who are working full-time and are too busy to keep their home clean. You don't need any qualifications for this, but you must be hard working and reliable, and you will probably be asked for references regarding your honesty. Cleaning jobs are usually part-time, and most cleaners work for several employers. Check out the local newspapers for advertisements.

Au pair

As an au pair, you are a curious blend of member of the family and staff. You will be treated as an older sister or brother, but you have to work 30 to 35 hours per week, looking after the children, maybe cleaning and cooking. In return, you get free accommodation with your own room and some pocket money, and the employers pay the fees for a college course one day per week.

Au pairs are between 18 and 27 years old. Most are young women, but the number of male au pairs is increasing. You don't need any experience or qualifications to apply, and au pair jobs are comparatively easy to find. Most au pair arrangements are for one year. You can apply directly to an employer, but it is advisable to use a reputable agency, either as soon as you arrive in Britain or while you are still in your home country. An agency can help you to find a family with similar interests.

Most au pair stays are rewarding, but problems do happen – such as the family expecting 72 hours slave labour every week and preventing you from attending your course, and lecherous fathers trying to gain access to your room at night. When such drastic problems occur, it can be difficult if you are on your own in a foreign country, without contacts and friends, and without speaking the language well. A good agency will check out the host families in advance and can help when matters go wrong.

The Home Office determines which countries can send au pairs to Britain. These include normally all European Union countries and currently also Croatia, Cyprus, Czech Republic, The Faeroes, Greenland, Hungary, Liechtenstein, Macedonia, Malta, Monaco, San Marino, Slovak Republic, Slovenia, Switzerland and Turkey.

'An au pair really does need to be understanding and patient, and enjoy some contact with children,' according to a spokesperson for Nightingale Nannies. 'Most au pair positions involve children, so if someone really does not get on with children or does not like working with them, au pairing is not for them. A good au pair would be prepared to try to fit in with the family life, be prepared to do things they would not normally do, such as certain aspects of housework or cooking. They may need to be flexible to be able to fit in with the family.'

Vivienne Colchester of ABC Au Pairs says, 'The au pair should be confident and reasonably outgoing, flexible to fit into the demands of a usually busy family life, happy and positive, independent, with an interest in other cultures, and active. Au pair work doesn't require specific training, but the au pair should be able to care for an interact with children, and have some relevant experience – for example, babysitting. She should be organised, tidy, able to do light housework, and able to use initiative, see what is needed without having to be told everything, and she should be speaking at least simple conversational English.'

'The ideal au pair has a happy disposition, who can take direction but also work on their own initiative, with lots of energy to throw themselves into the children's activities. A person with no experience with children should not try to work as an au pair,' says Nicola Quinn of Little Sprogs.

Maggie Dyer of The London au Pair & Nanny Agency describes the ideal au pair as 'happy, tolerant and flexible, ideally 19–25 years old, with younger siblings and plenty of babysitting experience.' She adds: 'If your English is better than basic level, and if you can commit yourself to stay nine to twelve months, this will help find a host family speedily. Don't apply as an au pair if you are planning to spend less than six months in Britain, if you are not interested in following a language (or some other) course, or if you smoke.

Nanny

A nanny is responsible for the children in their parents' absence. To find a job as a nanny, you must be either qualified or experienced, preferably both. Qualified nannies have usually attended a two-year college course, although shorter courses are sometimes acceptable. Alternatively, several years' experience as an au pair or mothers' help are often enough.

'At our agency, a nanny must hold a qualification in childcare,' explains the spokesperson of Nightingale Nannies. 'She is employed to do anything involving the children, e.g. childcare, cooking for the children, children's laundry and keeping the children's rooms clean and tidy. They do not do general housework. A live-in nanny would expect to earn around £180–£250 a week, depending on where the position is, experience and qualification. A daily nanny would expect similar amounts, but a good nanny can almost command her own fee with the right family.'

Nicola Quinn of Little Sprogs says, 'We recruit mostly nannies and maternity nurses. The candidates needs to have qualifications and substantial experience or both. The salary varies depending on age and experience but ranges from £150 net – £400 net and up to £570 gross for a maternity nurse.'

Maggie Dyer of The London Au Pair and Nanny Agency says, 'Nannies should have experience of caring for babies and young children on a full-time sole-charge basis. Up-to-date first aid skills including child and infant resuscitation and excellent English are essential.'

Mother's help

A spokesperson for Nightingale Nannies says, 'A mother's help may not have a formal qualification, but she will either have raised her own family, or have a proven track record with experience in this type of work. She will undertake any task usually done by the mother who runs the home. The jobs involves childcare, but is not restricted to this.'

'Mother's helps should love the idea of living with a family with young children and not be averse to housework. They earn a weekly net salary of between £150 to £180.'

Housekeeper

A typical housekeeper in a modern household will carry out light housekeeping duties such as dusting and tidying. He or she will do the laundry and ironing, organise the shopping, keep household accounts, take telephone messages, and take responsibility for security. Sometimes the housekeeper also does the cooking and the cleaning.

The housekeeper needs a mature, responsible personality, must be discreet, never talking about their employers. The ideal candidate has good references from previous household work. A cookery certificate and a driving licence help. A housekeeper earns between £120 and £280 weekly after tax and national insurance have been deducted. Housekeepers in the London area earn the highest salaries. Some housekeepers live out, others live in, with free accommodation provided by the employer.

Companion

A companion is often cook, housekeeper, carer and chauffeur at the same time. Companions provide the employer with sympathetic company, look after their laundry, drive them, care for them during illness, and look after their well-being, safety and security. Companions and their employers are usually both female. The companion can become close to her employer, because she is a friend as well as an employee, she goes out socially with her and they eat together. However, she should remember that she is still staff, and must not become too familiar. An agency will try to match employers with companions of similar interests and education. Live-in companions earn more than their live-out counterparts because they are 'on-call' even during their time off. If you have caring or nursing experience, you can get the better-paying companion jobs.

Chauffeur

Chauffeurs drive their employers to and from various places. They must also keep the car clean and well maintained, carrying out simple maintenance tasks. The chauffeur always gets out of the car first to open the door for employer or guests, taking care of briefcases, packages and shopping bags, and addresses their employers as Sir or Madam. Nowadays, this job is often combined with others, such as butler, valet, gardener or handyman, and it is fashionable for men to employ female chauffeurs.

The chauffeurs will normally wear a uniform, but if not, they must always look very presentable with jacket, tie and polished shoes. A chauffeur has excellent knowledge of the area, can always find a car parking space, is reliable and the soul of discretion. A clean driving licence with many years' experience is a must, but an Advanced Motorist Certificate and a Rolls Royce Certificate helps. Chauffeurs are paid £160–£200 net a week and can live out or live in.

Governess

A governess' job is to teach children in a private or family environment. Teaching experience and qualifications are a must. Most foreign governesses come from European or Commonwealth countries. They usually live in, and earn between £300 to £450 per week. Their employers are often wealthy families who have a reason for educating their children privately, perhaps because they feel that the tuition at state schools does not meet their ideals, or because their child has special requirements, perhaps on account of learning difficulties or a disability.

FINDING SECRETARIAL WORK

If you want to be a secretary in Britain, your best chance is in London, using an employment agency. Of course you must have excellent English and if you have a good command of other languages you can become a bilingual secretary.

Careers prospects for secretaries vary from sector to sector. Work in the areas of advertising, PR, publishing, marketing and the arts is regarded as glamorous and therefore not well paid. A good general secretary earns around £10,000 per year in Britain (around £12,000 a year in London). A bilingual secretary gets around £12,000–£15,000, but if she's well qualified and experienced and working in London she can earn £17,000 to £20,000.

For the top jobs, secretaries need to be good with computers, and able to use word processing, spreadsheet, desktop publishing and graphics software as well as the internet.

The best way to find secretarial employment is through specialist employment agencies.

Banking and insurance

Another 'glamorous' but better paid job is that of 'City secretary'. To work 'in the City' does not just mean to work in the centre of London, but to work in the financial industries based in the area around St Paul's, Bank and Mansion House.

A position in the City is automatically a job with a bank, an insurance or an investment firm. The most important criterion for 'City secretary' is her looks.

If you don't like this attitude, you'd better not apply for a City job. London offers many other options, and banks and insurance organisations pay well even outside the City.

Medical and legal

Secretaries with experience of working for doctors or solicitors are in demand and earn more than general secretaries.

Bilingual secretaries

'Bilingual secretary' is the term for a secretary who knows and uses languages. Sometimes the phrase 'trilingual secretary' is used for someone who speaks three languages, but usually bilingual is the word, however many languages you have.

The banking, finance, legal and media sectors offer the best prospects for bilingual secretaries. The languages most in demand are German, French, Spanish, Italian and Russian.

FINDING TEMPORARY WORK

Secretarial

Temporary work is popular in Britain. Many secretaries give up a permanent job to temp for a couple of years and gain experience in many industries. Enrol with one or several agencies. The demand for temporary secretaries is greatest in the summer months when the permanent secretaries are on holiday.

Agriculture

During the summer and autumn it is easy to find work, picking strawberries, apples, grapes and hops. In the spring you may be able to work as a lambing assistant. These jobs last usually for jut a couple of weeks, sometimes for a month or two, then you move on to another farm where you harvest something else. Sometimes, but not often, basic accommodation is provided.

Farmers advertise for workers in local newspapers, or put up cards in village shop windows. They won't consider applicants who are still living abroad. But if you live locally, understand enough English to follow instructions, and are willing to work hard, you'll probably get a job.

Hotel and catering

From May to September there are vacancies for chambermaids, waiting staff, receptionists, cleaners and kitchen staff in hotels and restaurants, especially along the coast. Restaurants all over the UK also take on temporary staff during December to cope with the Christmas business. Kitchen work and chambermaiding are the best possibilities if your English is not good and if you don't have any catering qualifications or experience.

Shops

You are most likely to find a temp job as a sales assistant, on a supermarket checkout or filling shelves during December (Christmas purchases) and January (end-of-season sales).

DOING VOLUNTARY WORK

If you can't find a proper job, you should consider taking on **unpaid work** for a while. Once you have proved that you are able to work in the UK, British employers will be more willing to take you on.

A period of voluntary work will look good in your CV. It gives

THE BEST SEASONS TO FIND TEMP JOBS	Jan	Feb	Mar	Apr	May	Jun	Jul	Aug	Sep	Oct	Nov	Dec
In **offices** (for example, typing)						✓	✓	✓	✓			
In **shops** (for example, stocking shelves)	✓										✓	✓
In **hotels** (for example chambermaid)						✓	✓	✓	✓			
In **restaurants** (for example, waiter)					✓	✓	✓	✓	✓			✓
In **vineyards** (grape harvest)							✓	✓	✓			
On **farms** (picking strawberries)						✓	✓	✓	✓	✓		
On **farms** (hop picking)								✓	✓			
On **farms** (apple harvest)								✓	✓	✓		

Please note: Vacancies for temporary and seasonal occur only (or mainly) in certain regions. For example, most office jobs are in cities, most hotel jobs in tourism areas, and agricultural jobs depend on the produce grown in the region.

Fig. 2. Chart of seasonal temp jobs.

you the chance to practise the English language in a work environment and to learn new skills.

There are almost always unpaid vacancies in the social services sector, in charity shops, or with environmental organisations, for example creating wildlife habitats.

Ask around in the neighbourhood, contact your borough council, the library or the Women's Institute.

CHECKLIST

1. Which marketable skills do I have?
2. Are they in demand in Britain?
3. Do I want to work in the job for which I'm trained, or am I interested in doing something different?
4. Is my English good enough for the work I want to do?
5. Would it help me if my first job in Britain was 'live in'?
6. How much would I have to earn to achieve the living standard I've been used to in my home country?

CASE STUDIES

May gets unexpected promotion

'My friend Michelle and I decided to give up our sales jobs in Australia and travel around the world for a couple of years when we were 28. Our first destination was London. We found it easy to get jobs as chambermaids, and chose to work for two different hotels in the same road. The one where I worked was quite a big one, whereas Michelle's place was more a pension than a hotel. To my surprise I was promoted to head chambermaid within two weeks, with a pay rise. I thought my boss was joking. But the head chambermaid had left at short notice, and I was considered the only one able to take on the added responsibility which involved dealing with problems, managing rotas, and dealing with complaints. Some of the other chambermaids were not mature enough; others were not conscientious enough in their work, and some didn't speak enough English. I've been here for three months now and I enjoy the job. I'm considering changing my career: there seem to be excellent prospects in the hotel industry. But Michelle keeps nagging, she wants to see Paris next.'

Monika throws the towel

'I trained as an industrial manager in Germany. When I was 23, I came to London, hoping to find a job which would help me to improve my English. But the agency with which I registered classed me as 'kitchen staff', simply because my grammar was not perfect.

'After three days of peeling potatoes and drying plates for little money I had had enough. I literally 'threw the towel' as we say in Germany, and went to another agency.

'There the consultant was impressed with my qualifications, and encouraged me to practise typing in their office every day until I achieved a satisfactory speed. Then he found me a job as secretary with a bank. The bank paid for me to study better English at night school. After a year, I was promoted dealings clerk.'

Laurenz quits the job

'It was quite easy to find an au pair job in Britain – I applied through an agency in Paris who sorted everything out for me. When I arrived at the airport, the father of the host family picked me up. But I hated the job! I felt used. I suppose I had the wrong attitude for an au pair. I had to look after the children, bath them, wash up – that's not the sort of thing you like to do when you're an 18-year-old girl who has just escaped home.

'After three months, I took my weekly pay of £25 and my suitcase and left. I bought a newspaper to scan job adverts, I slept in the street. For three days I went jobhunting every day from 8.30 in the morning to 8.30 in the evening. Then, through sheer persistence, I landed a job as a waitress. I stayed there for nine months. That was eight years ago. I have since worked as an advertising sales representative, and now I'm working in a bank.'

Tejal becomes self-employed

'I was a mechanical engineer in the United States. When I came to live in Britain with my husband, I could not find work in my skills area. All mechanical engineering jobs I applied for were considered 'high security' and unaccessible for foreigners. In the end, I decided to turn my hobby into cash. I became a belly dance teacher and performer. This is going really well. I'm teaching belly dance classes in many places in Buckinghamshire and beyond. Being a foreigner helps, especially as I'm half Indian. Never mind that the type of dance I'm teaching is Middle Eastern, not Indian, and that I learnt it in New York. My students often say "You're so exotic", they are really envious. They prefer an "exotic" teacher to an Englishwoman.'

Zinga's wife finds a job for him

'In Tunisia, I worked as a supervisor in a hotel, and as a percussionist. My wife found me a job in Tunbridge Wells where her family live, as a restaurant supervisor. I enjoy it because it involves communicating with customers and staff, and gives me the opportunity to improve my English, but customers can be annoyingly fussy sometimes.'

Carina works as a dancer

'I was working with a big annual multi media, multi cultural event in Gothenburg in Sweden. After studying in London, the first job I found was performing dance.'

Lynne finds it difficult

'I soon discovered that an American BA in History was good for little more than covering up a patch of scuffed wallpaper! I work in computers now. The UK is just as starved for high-tech workers as the rest of the world, so if you are a computer expert, you shouldn't have a problem. The English central and southern counties are the best places to go for high pay in the computing sector.'

POINTS TO CONSIDER

1. What will you do if you arrive in Britain and cannot find work in your skills area, or if you lose the job you have come for? What are your contingency plans?

2. How will your stay in Britain fit in with your long term career plan?

3. Would you consider working in a different sector and a different job? If yes: temporarily, or permanently? Which sector, which job, and which career would you consider?

6

Applying for a Job

Don't expect it to be easier to find a job in Britain than in your home country. It will probably be more difficult, because most employers prefer taking on staff who are familiar with the working environment and the language. However, your nationality may be a bonus. Nationals of some countries have a reputation for being well trained and skilled in particular jobs. There are many Norwegian people working in the oil industry; Luxembourg nationals in banking and finance; people from Malaysia and the Philippines in domestic employment; Italians in the hotels and restaurants; Australian nannies and young New Zealanders financing their European trip as chambermaids.

WRITING APPLICATION LETTERS

Most employers prefer typed application letters to handwritten ones (see Figure 4). Begin your letter with Dear Ms (or Mr, Mrs, Miss) X. If you don't know the name of the person who reads it, start with 'Dear Sir or Madam'. Don't just say 'Dear Sir' – a female personnel manager may find this rude.

Good opening sentences are 'I have read, with interest, your advertisement in xxx magazine' or 'I am writing to enquire if you are likely to have a vacancy for a xxxxx in the near future'.

British employers place great emphasis on CVs, but your application letter is a sales tool as well. It should therefore include your major 'sales argument', the most important reason why you are the right person for the job.

Your letter should fit on one white A4 page and look well presented, without typing errors. If English is a second language for you, it's a good idea to write the application letter in draft form first and let a British friend have a look at it before you type out the final version.

Sabine Schmidt, 2 Wax Road, Slushton, AB1 2CD.
Tel: 00000/00000

Ms Clare
Personnel Manager
The International PR Company
1 London Road
Oakhurst AA1 1AA

1 February 200X

Dear Ms Clare,

I have read, with interest, your advertisement in the "Oakhurst & Slushton Chronicle", and I would like to apply for the position of bilingual secretary/PA.

I have worked as a secretary and personal assistant for many years, and I am fully familiar with all aspects of secretarial work. I speak and write three European languages fluently. As you can see from my enclosed CV, German is my native tongue, and I lived and worked a year in France as well. In 199X I joined my husband in the UK. I have been working as a temporary secretary since then.

I look forward to hearing from you.

Yours sincerely

Sabine Schmidt
Sabine Schmidt

Fig. 3. Sample application letter.

CV: Sabine Schmidt

Address: 2 Wax Road, Slushton, AB1 2CD.
Tel. 00000/00000
Born: 20 July 1964, Stuttgart (Germany)

Secretarial skills: copy typing 80wpm
audio typing 50wpm
shorthand 60wpm

Computing skills: word processing (WordPerfect, Word for Windows, IBM Displaywrite)
desktop publishing (Ventura, Pagemaker, Quark Xpress)
some spreadsheet experience

Languages: German (native tongue)
English (fluent)
French (fluent)
Spanish (basic – 1 year at evening class)

Work history:

Currently	**Temporary Secretary** with TopSecs in Slushton.
1993–1995	**Bilingual Marketing Secretary**, Bauer & Co OHG, Stuttgart. Duties included: all the company's bilingual correspondence, making appointments for sales representatives, telephone liaison, general office administration. Reason for leaving: to live and work in Britain.
1983–1993	**Junior Secretary**, after two years promoted to **Personal Assistant**. Maier GmbH. Duties included: Keeping the managing director's diary, preparing presentations and conferences, audio and copy typing, shorthand, desktop publishing, correspondence in German, English and French. Reason for leaving: I wanted more opportunity to use my language skills.
1982–1983	**Au Pair** with family in Paris.

Secondary and further education:

1980–1982	Secretarial College, Stuttgart, Languages studied: German, English, French.
1974–1980	Realschule (secondary school), school leaving certificate Mittlere Reife (GCSE 'O' level equivalent).

Interests: Skiing, volleyball, reading, amateur dramatics.

Fig. 4. Sample CV.

WRITING THE PERFECT CV

Your CV should contain your name, address, date and place of birth, education, employment history, skills and interests. Most employers prefer it in tabular format (see Figure 5).

List your **jobs** in reverse chronological order, starting with the most recent one, and going back from there. This is because the employer is most interested in what you have been doing recently rather than in the jobs you held years ago. Write down the job titles, the name of the company, how long you stayed with them, as well as 'duties included: . . .' and 'reason for leaving: . . .'.

It is a good idea to emphasise **duties** which are similar to those of the job for which you apply. If you apply for different types of jobs, have differently phrased CVs, emphasising the relevant skills, experiences and interests.

Think carefully about your 'reasons for leaving' and edit them if necessary.

Reasons for leaving which prospective employers like are:
- 'to learn new skills'
- 'to take on more responsibility'
- 'better promotion prospects'.

Reasons which they don't mind include:
- 'to cut down on commuting time'
- 'to live nearer my family'
- 'to earn a better salary'
- 'because of the company's uncertain future'
- 'redundancy'.

Reasons which ring warning bells are:
- 'boredom'
- 'clash of personalities with boss/colleagues'
- 'don't really know'.

Include your secondary and higher **education**, the years you spent at the school/college/university, the subjects you studied and the qualifications you achieved. Nobody is interested in your primary school education.

If necessary, provide job titles and qualifications in your native language, with a brief explanation in English in brackets.

For example: 'Verwaltungsfachangestellte (administration manager)'.

SITUATIONS VACANT

Temporary farm workers needed. To assist in picking and packaging of fruit. No experience needed but applicants have to be over 16 years of age. Camping facilities also available. For details, contact Mr E. George or Mrs S. Miller on 0000 0000 (answerphone).

Assistant Cook, £5 per hour, 21 hours per week including alternate weekends. Applicants must have experience of cooking for 50+ people and a Food Hygiene Certificate. Mature applicant preferred. Please apply in writing, giving details of previous experience, to: The Oakhurst Home, Oakhurst Road, Oakhurst AA1 2BB.

House sitter required for two week period to look after house + animals. Please apply in writing, giving details and reference, to: 49 Upper Snodington Lane, Oakhurst AA2 1CC.

 Green Leaves Gardening Contractors

Assistant gardeners/groundsmen needed, both part-time and full-time, salary negotiable, at least 21 hours a week.
Contact: E. Stone, Green Leaves Gardening Contractors, Turf Lane, Thornton. TU3 SS1.

Wanted:
Bilingual secretary/PA with fluent French. Additional European language an advantage. Must have exp. and at least 60wpm typing, plus rusty shorthand.

 Apply to: Ms Clare, Personnel Manager, The International PR Company, 1 London Road, Oakhurst AA1 1AA.

High Hill Ski Club

Part-time *race instructor* required, to teach slalom technique, and other racing skills. Eight hours a week at most required. Evenings only. Applicants must have experience in both racing and teaching.

Please write giving details of skills to The Personnel Manager, High Hill Ski Club, Wax Road, Slushton.

Fig. 5. Sample 'jobs vacant' advertisements.

There are small businesses which specialise in writing or rewriting CVs. If you are uncertain about how to write a CV so that it has maximum impact, or if English is a second language for you, or if you can't type or don't have access to a typewriter or computer, it may be an idea to use their services.

Type your CV on one side of white A4 paper. For a holiday or temp job, your CV will probably be just one or two pages long. A secretarial CV is likely to be about three pages, and managers with many years' experience may use more pages, although an over-long CV may put off many employers.

LOOKING AT ADVERTISEMENTS

National newspapers are a good source of executive and managerial vacancies. They have some special job supplements which deal with one industry sector at a time. For example, *The Guardian* contains advertising and media jobs on Saturdays and Mondays.

If you are interested in a specific sector, consult the specialist press – for example, the *UK Press Gazette* for journalists, the *Times Educational Supplement* for teachers.

See Figure 6 for some sample job advertisments.

USING THE JOBCENTRE

Almost every town has a **Jobcentre**. This is a government office where you can go to find out about jobs available. It displays local jobs on cards on notice-boards under sector headings, such as 'Nursing', 'Office', 'Building'. Just go in and look around. If you see a job which matches your skills and interests, write down the reference number and ask a member of staff for more details. They can tell you where and how to apply.

You can also register with the Jobcentre by filling in a form with the type of job you are looking for. When a suitable vacancy comes up, they'll contact you. But don't rely on this; if you are looking for a job, it's a good idea to drop into the Jobcentre at least once a week.

The services of the Jobcentre are free of charge and you don't need an appointment to go there. They are particularly good for manual, low-paid and temporary work, although they place many skilled labourers as well. Managers and executives are seldom recruited through the Jobcentre.

You can find out where the nearest Jobcentre is by looking at a phone book or by asking in the library or any government office.

GOING TO THE INTERVIEW

Dress smartly when you go to the interview. Women should wear a suit in a discreet colour, such as grey or navy blue. Wear make-up, but avoid large jewellery and perfume.

Questions for which you should be prepared are:

- Why did you leave your home country?
- What are you running away from?
- Why did you leave your last job?

If you are indeed 'running away' from something (poverty, a messy divorce, a criminal record, an unhappy love affair, pushy parents, an arranged marriage or whatever) don't admit it!

State clearly that you came to Britain because you want to be in this country. Repeat it if necessary. The interviewer will ask you why. Here are some reasons which will be accepted by employers:

- 'To learn/improve my language skills.'

- 'To be with my family/friends/fiancé(e)/husband/wife.'

- 'Because I like the country' (be prepared to give details).

- 'Because I admire the British people' (this is the most successful especially with older interviewers – but use it only if you can keep a straight face).

- 'I want to learn from the British who have such a high standard of skills and technology in this field' (if you believe it yourself).

- 'I enjoy sharing my skills' (only if your knowledge and skills are superior and the job you seek involves training your colleagues).

APPLYING WHILE STILL ABROAD

It is difficult to find a job if you apply from abroad. Employers prefer to hire someone whom they can interview in person. There are exceptions, of course: families seeking au pairs will usually trust an agency to do the interviewing abroad and find a suitable person. Sometimes UK employers cannot find staff with the right qualifications (for example, languages) and may use international agencies or advertise in the foreign press.

Of course you can study British newspapers and magazines while you are still abroad. But there is a time problem: the newspaper will probably arrive in your country after several days' delay, and your application letter has to travel a longer way. By the time it arrives on the personnel manager's desk, the job may have gone.

If you are an EU/EEA citizen, you can register with the employment service in your own country which will help you find a job in Britain. There is a partnership between all employment services in the EU and EEA to support the free movement of workers. The system is called the EURES (European Employment Services) Network.

REGISTERING WITH RECRUITMENT AGENCIES

If you have special skills or qualifications, you will probably find a better job by using a recruitment agency. Some agencies deal with all types of jobs, but in the cities most agencies specialise in one or several types of jobs or industry sectors. For example, there are agencies for catering or for healthcare staff.

To find recruitment agencies, look up the *Yellow Pages* under 'Employment Agencies and Consultants'. You can also write to the Federation of Recruitment and Employment Services Limited (FRES). This is a trade association of recruitment agencies which may be able to recommend a suitable agency for your line of work. Their address is FRES, 36–38 Mortimer Street, London WIN 7RB. Please enclose a stamped addressed envelope or an International Reply Coupon.

It is also worth studying the pages of the specialist press for the sector in which you want to work.

Some agencies prefer you to make an appointment, but most are happy for you to walk in. You will be interviewed by a consultant and asked to fill in a form. Take a copy of your CV with you and leave it with the agency. Very occasionally, an agent may ask for references or photos. You might have to take a test of some sort.

The services of recruitment agents are free to the jobhunter. The agency gets a fee from the employer when you are offered a contract.

It is therefore in their interest to find you a job. The consultant will contact you when there is a suitable vacancy, and ask you if you want them to forward your application. If prospective employers are interested, they will invite you to an interview.

However, don't rely on the consultant to inform you. Keep dropping in or phoning your consultant at least every other week. Consultants have the habit of forgetting candidates who don't keep in touch. Don't let that happen to you.

There is nothing to stop you from registering with several agencies simultaneously. Especially if you are in London and want to be a secretary, you can register with a dozen or more agencies to increase your chances.

The acknowledged best source for addresses of agencies is the monthly magazine *The Lady*. You can also consult *Yellow Pages* and the newspaper *Overseas Jobs Express*. A long established agency which places domestic staff who have a work permit is Park Lane Nannies.

Park Lane Nannies
This agency deals with nannies, au pairs and governesses. Contact: Park Lane Nannies, 22 Upper Maudlin Street, Bristol BS2 8DJ.

Executive recruitment agencies
Agencies for executive and managerial positions usually seek to fill specific vacancies for the employers. You can find their addresses when they advertise vacancies in the national press. If they advertise a position for which you don't have the right skills, but which is related to your qualifications and experience, chances are that they may have a suitable vacancy in the future. Send them your CV on spec and suggest they keep it for future reference.

Secretarial agencies
There are many secretarial agencies, especially in London. Some specialise in certain industry sectors, others are general. They don't normally welcome applications from abroad, but once you are in the country, you can register with them.

If you live in London and are after secretarial work, you can pick up magazines aimed at job-hunting secretaries. These include: *Nine To Five*, *Girl About Town*, *Ms London*. Once a week, they are distributed at main underground stations and if you see them piled up at your station entrance, take a copy. It's free. Recruitment agencies use them to advertise their latest vacancies. The magazines also contain some general reading matter – interviews with handsome film stars, beauty and fashion tips, film reviews. A secretary will almost certainly be checked for her typing speed, combined perhaps with speedwriting, audio and proofreading skills. Take care when you do the typing test: keyboards differ from country to country, and it is possible that one or two keys are not in the place where you expect them to be. Some agencies offer extra services, such as rewriting your CV, or teaching you new wordprocessing programmes. Some do this free of charge, others ask for a fee. If you can learn a new skill for free and have the time, take the opportunity. The more skills you have, the easier it will be to find a job.

The two following agencies encourage foreign applicants. For further addresses, refer to the Useful Addresses section:

Cavell Bilingual Recruitment, 26 Goodge Street, London W1P 1FG.
Boyce Bilingual, Suite 4F, Liberty House, 222 Regent Street, London W1R 5DE.

USEFUL ABBREVIATIONS

wpm	words per minute (typing/shorthand speed)
s/h	shorthand
temp	temporary
perm	permanent
MD	managing director
WP	wordprocessing
DTP	desktop publishing
PA	personal assistant
pa	per annum (wages per year)
exp	experience.

CHECKLIST

1. Have I decided whether I will apply from my home country, or whether it is better to go to Britain and start job-hunting when I'm there?

2. Have I found out which employment agencies are likely to have vacancies for me?

3. Which newspapers or magazines are likely to carry 'jobs vacant' advertisements for the work I want to do?

4. Do I have a neatly presented CV? Is it in correct English?

5. Do I have photocopies of references and certificates at hand, in case they are required?

CASE STUDIES

Monica meets prejudice

'I was a celebrated author and playwright in my home country, Korea. I came down to earth with a bang here in Britain. I knew that these specific writing skills would not be in demand, but I was not prepared for the reality: employers just didn't believe that I had any skills.

'I remember a typical interviewer: "Do you speak any English?" Of course I did speak English, otherwise I would not have been to the interview.

'The next question: "Did you do any work in Korea?" I thought if I told her the truth, she would not believe me. So I mentioned the job for which I had trained, and qualified, and in which I had worked before going freelance as a writer. I said "Yes, I was a teacher."

'The interviewer just mocked me: "So, so, you were a teacher, were you?" She would not even consider that I could have had a qualified and responsible job. Her behaviour was so condescending. She mocked me. This hurt. She would never have reacted this way if an Englishwoman had said she was a teacher.'

Christine edits her CV

'When I came to the UK, I applied for a job as a journalist – I had been deputy editor of a magazine in Germany. All the rejection letters said the same: "We are impressed with your skills and qualifications, but we are afraid we would not consider employing a journalist whose native tongue is not English".

'So I applied as a bilingual secretary, for which I was also qualified. Getting the first job was difficult. I started jobhunting on the south coast where I had friends, but I should have gone to London where the jobs are.

'I registered with 50 agencies, and needed seven weeks to find the first job. It was easy to find follow-on jobs as a secretary or linguist. 'After a year, I tried again as a journalist. This time, my application letters didn't say "I am German, but speak and write English fluently" but simply "I have perfect German". I even edited my CV, dropping all German names and places. Now it just stated that I had studied at business college, trained to be a publisher, and worked as deputy editor of a women's magazine – it didn't say where.

'This worked beautifully. I replied to advertisements and was invited to interviews. Once I was there, I could no longer hide my nationality, but I had the opportunity to demonstrate my skills and argue my case. I got a job which had been advertised in *The Guardian* as "Experienced deputy editor wanted for magazines – second European language an advantage". Well, I did have the European language, didn't I?'

Lynne uses the Jobcentre

'At first I made use of the Jobcentres in Aberdeen. Prospective employers post cards on billboards detailing what they're looking for; you take down reference numbers for the ones you're interested in, and Jobcentre staff will provide you with more detail, the application forms, and occasionally they help with applying if you make an appointment. It's worth checking in to the Jobcentre once or twice a week to look for new postings. These tend to be mostly entry-level jobs, though.

POINTS TO CONSIDER

1. If you are applying for several types of job: would it be best to have several different CVs? If yes, which are the points to emphasise in which CV? Which points are better left out?

2. Prepare a strategy for your jobhunting in the UK. Plan in advance which steps you are going to take, and when. For example:
   Week 1: Have my CV professionally rewritten. Register with at least five secretarial employment agencies. Study *Yellow Pages* to find addresses of potential employers. Study job advertisements in national newspapers. *Week 2*: Register with five more agencies. Send out at least ten on spec applications.

7

Handling the Paperwork

During your first few days, weeks or months in the UK you will be busy with a lot of paperwork. You may have to:

- apply for a residence permit, if required (see page 24)

- decide which name you are going to use

- register with a doctor and a dentist, as soon as you have decided where to live (see page 157)

- open a bank account

- register for National Insurance

- register with the local council office

- apply for a television licence

- exchange your driving licence

- apply for a library card (see page 121)

- register with your embassy.

REGISTERING FOR NATIONAL INSURANCE

As soon as you arrive in Britain, you should register for **National Insurance** (NI). For this, you have to visit your nearest Social Security Contributions office. You will find the address in your local telephone book under either 'Social Security' or 'Contributions Agency'. Take your passport or identity card with you.

A few days or weeks later, you will be sent a card with your NI number on it. Keep the card safe, and memorise or write down your number – you will need it all the time in Britain, whenever you have to fill in a form.

Most people working in Britain have to pay National Insurance contributions. The exception is people on a very low income. How much you pay depends on your income. If you have a job, your employer will deduct your NI contributions automatically.

NI contributions entitle you to retirement pension, unemployment benefit, maternity allowance *etc,* but only under certain circumstances. Some other social security benefits, such as income support, don't depend on previous NI contributions. If you want to find out if you are entitled to a benefit, you have to contact the 'Benefits Agency'.

Check in your phone book – there may be freefone numbers, and helplines in different languages. Your local post office may have booklets and brochures on National Insurance and Social Security.

CHANGING YOUR NAME

In Britain, you don't have to use the name under which you lived in your home country. You may want to choose a different name, for example because your real name is too difficult for British tongues to pronounce.

There is no paperwork involved, no permissions, nothing. However, the first few months can involve some explaining, because you have to prove that you are who you say.

For example, when opening a bank account you have to show your passport (which contains, of course, your 'old' name). It's OK to say 'I'm Johann Schmidt, but in this country I'm known as John Smith'.

Please note: although the use of a name of your choice is accepted for everyday life, this does not change your name in the eyes of the law. When filling in official forms, you should write under the heading 'names': 'Johann Schmidt, also known as John Smith'.

Your choice of name in Britain does not change your name in your home country, either. For example, if you want to renew your passport, it will be in your old name. European passports have a space for 'pseudonym'; if you can prove that you have used your new name for work purposes for a while, you can have it entered as a pseudonym.

For details on how to change your name officially and for good, contact the embassy or high commission of your home country.

EXCHANGING YOUR DRIVING LICENCE

You can use the driving licence from your home country during your first year in Britain. After that, you have to obtain a British driving licence. For this, you may have to take a driving test.

It is easier if you are a national of a European Union country or of Australia, Barbados, British Virgin Islands, Republic of Cyprus, Finland, Hong Kong, Japan, Kenya, Malta, New Zealand, Singapore or Zimbabwe. You can exchange your driving licence for a British one but have to pay a fee for this.

You can pick up the application form for the exchange of your licence at the post office.

For information about driving licences contact: Customer Enquiries Unit, DVLC, Swansea SA6 7JL. Tel: (01792) 772151, Fax: (01792) 783071.

APPLYING FOR A TELEVISION LICENCE

If you want to watch television in your home, you must pay for a television licence.

Obtain a form from your post office, fill it in and pay the fee. You will get a fee stamp on it, confirming the payment, and can use it for a year. It is also possible to pay in monthly or quarterly instalments by direct debit.

A fleet of detector vans can track down unlicensed users. Watching TV without the right licence is a criminal office, and you risk a fine of up to £1,000.

If you want to find out more, contact: TV Licensing, Barton House, Bristol BS98 1TL. Tel: (0117) 9230130.

REGISTERING WITH THE LOCAL COUNCIL

In addition to income tax, which is deducted from your salary, you will also have to pay tax to your local council. This tax has caused a lot of protests in recent years and has been reshuffled, re-organised and re-named to pacify people. You may hear it called poll tax, council tax or community tax. Who has to pay this tax and how much changes all the time.

It's difficult to predict what the position will be when you arrive in Britain. Maybe all house owners have to pay it and the rate depends on the value of the building. Maybe it's all householders, regardless of the value of the building and the number of the occupants. Maybe it's calculated at a fixed rate per head, with reductions for the unemployed and for students.

One thing is certain, however: if you don't pay, you are in trouble. Sometimes your landlord or landlady will obtain a registration form for you. Otherwise you must find out by yourself what the current requirements for registration and tax are. The best place to enquire is the nearest county council or borough council. Staff are usually friendly and helpful when it comes to guiding new residents through the jungle of bureaucracy. There is also a leaflet called *Help with your council tax*.

The UKCOSA publishes a leaflet *Council tax* (see Useful Addresses).

REGISTERING WITH YOUR EMBASSY

Most embassies don't keep lists of their nationals resident in Britain. Others recommend or insist that you register with them, which allows them to keep statistics and to take action in an emergency (for example, evacuation in the case of a civil war). Phone your embassy or high commission in London to find out if you should register.

CHECKLIST

1. Have I registered for National Insurance and obtained an NI number?

2. Have I registered with a local doctor's surgery (and see Chapter 15)?

3. Have I registered with a dentist?

4. Have I registered with my embassy (if appropriate)?

5. Have I registered with my local council office?

6. Have I opened a bank account?

7. Have I obtained a library card?

8. Have I applied for a television licence (if desired)?

9. Have I applied for a UK driving licence (if relevant)?

10. Have I applied for a vehicle registration (if relevant)?

CASE STUDY

Erik opens a bank account

'Opening a bank account for my monthly salary presented unexpected difficulties. The bank insisted on seeing not only my Swedish passport, but also a reference from someone who held an account with them and who had known me for at least six months.

'This was impossible, because I had been in the UK for only a month. But I needed a bank account, otherwise I could not cash the monthly cheques from my employers. I could not wait for six months!

'I explained the situation to the bank clerk, and offered to provide another form of reference instead – for example from the manager of the bank where I had had an account for ten years. But the clerk said rules were rules and sent me away. Dispirited, I told the tale in the office. My new colleagues were sympathetic. One of them, who had an account with the bank in question, was willing to bend the truth and claimed that she had known me for six months.

'Armed with her reference, I returned to the bank. The clerk didn't show any surprise but opened the account for me.'

8

Finding Accommodation

TO RENT OR BUY?

About two-thirds of British households live in a home they own. To own a house or a flat is considered desirable and normal. Most Britons accept rented accommodation only as a temporary solution – maybe while they are waiting to find the right house to buy, or until a divorce has come through, or while studying in another town.

As well as being a home, a house is often regarded as an investment which increases in value and can be sold after a few years at a profit (or so the owners hope). But unless you expect to stay for five years or more, it is probably not worth the work, administrative hassle and expense to buy a house.

You will probably find there are more houses available to buy than to rent. Rents can be astronomical, especially in London and the southeast.

LOOKING AT THE HOUSING MARKET

In the 1970s and 1980s, almost everyone wanted to buy a house. They chose the most expensive house they could afford, regarding it as an investment which would increase in value.

The future, as they imagined it, was idyllic: every few years they would sell their house, and with the profit buy an even bigger one. They would continue to 'trade up' until they lived in greatest possible comfort.

To calculate how much they could afford to pay, they looked at their salary expectations, and estimated that they could pay back so much per month on the mortgage. Many went one step further and decided to take in a lodger. The lodger, they assumed, would pay them as much rent as they had for the mortgage. Thus they could buy and own a house while paying hardly anything for it.

When the property bubble burst

Of course the bubble had to burst (everyone expected it to, except the British). To start with, there was a shortage of lodgers. Who in their right mind would pay a monthly rent as a monthly mortgage repayment for a family house?

They all wanted to jump on the bandwagon and get rich. Nobody wanted to make someone else rich.

Then came the recession: people lost their jobs, or at least didn't get the salary rises they had expected. They could not afford the huge mortgages any more. Now they tried to sell their expensive houses and buy smaller, cheaper ones. But there were few buyers for the costly mansions, so they were stuck. The housing market broke down, many houses went gone down in price by 20 per cent or more, and owners had to sell at a substantial loss. Today the housing market has stablised.

Estate agents report that large luxurious houses are the most difficult to sell (and can therefore be bought at a reasonable price), whereas cottages with two to three bedrooms and small terraced homes are more difficult to find.

Houses in and around London and in the southeast are far more expensive than in the north.

BUYING A HOUSE

If you want to buy a house, you contact an estate agent to discuss your requirements and the price you can afford. Estate agents can also explain the principles of how to get a mortgage. In Scotland, many solicitors act as estate agents, and wherever you live in the UK, you will need a solicitor to handle the paperwork involved in house purchase.

Estate agents display photos and brief descriptions of properties in their shop windows and their offices. You can go window shopping to get an idea of how much a suitable house would cost.

If you are able to pay cash, or can arrange a mortgage quickly, you can make an offer below the asking price. The owners will probably be relieved to sell their house quickly.

Many local newspapers publish weekly property supplements with estate agents' advertisements and editorial descriptions of houses. These supplements are free.

Houses are described by the number of bedrooms (not rooms). So a 'five bedroom house' can have six rooms or twelve. You'll have to read the small print to find out if there is a dining room, a lounge, a study, a games room *etc.*

FINDING A BEDSIT

If you are studying, or have no money to invest, or don't intend to stay long, you will prefer to rent accommodation. Look at some of the local newspapers; they carry 'accommodation vacant' advertisements (see Figure 9).

You can also ask an estate agent. Most of them deal in rented property as well. However, the agent may charge a service fee when you accept accommodation. If they ask you to pay a fee upfront, refuse. You should pay only on success.

Rented accommodation usually comes complete with furniture; unfurnished places can be difficult to find.

Students and single people often choose **flatshare** arrangements where several people rent the flat together. Each gets a room, but they all use the bathroom and kitchen. Each pays a share of the rent and the bills. If you consider a flatshare, choose only one with one or two other people. If seven students share a flat, there will be queues outside the toilet every morning, and there will never be any hot water left when you want to take a bath.

You can also rent a room with a family and use their bathroom and kitchen. Many families who have difficulty keeping up their mortgage repayments make one room available for a lodger. Sometimes these arrangements include breakfast or another meal. These rooms are often called 'bedsits', although strictly speaking a bedsit should be almost self-contained, with its own washing and cooking facilities.

Expect to pay around £65 per week including bills for a room in a flatshare or with a family in London. For this price, you should get a small to medium-sized room, practically furnished, in a clean house, within walking distance of an underground station.

STAYING AT THE INTERNATIONAL STUDENT HOUSE

If you are looking for budget accommodation in central London in a relatively safe environment, consider the International Student House in Great Portland Street.

'Long stay accommodation is only for students, but anyone is welcome to stay as short-stay guests,' says marketing assistant,

Shelly Roberts. The hostel caters primarily for international students, but also accommodates UK students and non-student visitors. As well as accommodation and meals, it provides a cultural, social and recreational programme for 365 days of the year. Facilities include a Cyber Café, a Fitness Centre, three bars, a travel club, societies and an outlet of Travelcuts. The house was founded by Mary Trevelyan in 1965 as a private club and is registered as a charity.

Prices per person per night (short stay):
Bed in a multi-bedded room, no breakfast	£9.99
Bed in a four-bedded room with breakfast	£17.50
Bed in a three-bedded room with breakfast	£20.00
Bed in a twin-bedded room with breakfast	£22.50
Single room with breakfast	£31.00
En-suite single room with breakfast	£33.00
Bed in en-suite twin room with breakfast	£25.50

You'll be charged a deposit which you get back when you return your keys before 10am the following day.

Special short-stay weekly rates from September to May
Single room with washbasin per person per week	£187.60
Twin room with washbasin per person per week	£140

Long-stay accommodation (minimum three months, for students only, no meals)
Single room: £140.30 per week for the first four weeks, thereafter £89.60 per week
Bed in a twin room: £81.75 per week for the first four weeks, thereafter £68.81 per week
Bed in a treble room: £63.42 for the first four weeks, thereafter £54.46 per week
Bed in a dormitory: £48.72 for the first four weeks, thereafter £42.48 per week.

In addition, you have to pay a booking fee of £25, a membership fee of £29m and alumni membership of £15. You get discounts on meals in the self-service restaurant. You also have to pay a security deposit of £350 which you will get back when you depart leaving the room in a good condition.

Address (postal): 1 Park Crescent, Regent's Park, London W1B 1SH. Entrance address: 229 Great Portland Street, Regent's Park, London W1W 5PN. Tel: (020) 7631 8300, Fax: (020) 7631 8315, e-mail: *general@ish.org.uk www.ish.org.uk*

CHECKLIST FOR RENTING ACCOMMODATION

1. Is it large enough?
2. Of which rooms and facilities do I have exclusive use?
3. Which rooms and facilities do I share with others? (Garden, bath, shower, communal room, television, washing machine, telephone?)
4. If rooms and facilities are shared, can I use them only at specified times? Are these times convenient for me?
5. How much storage space can I use in the kitchen?
6. How much is the rent per week?
7. Do I pay weekly or monthly?
8. Will there be a rent book?
9. Do I have to pay a deposit?
10. Do I have to pay an agent's fee?
11. Which bills are there to pay (electricity, gas, water, council tax, telephone, TV licence)? Are they included in the rent? If not, how much are they likely to cost? If I'm sharing accommodation, how will my share be calculated?
13. Is the furniture practical for me?
14. Can the rooms be heated in winter?
15. Do I like the people with whom I'm sharing the flat? Do I trust them?
16. Where is the nearest underground or railway station or bus stop? Where do the trains and buses go, and how frequently?
17 How far is it to my place of work, the nearest shops, the library, the nearest park, the church/mosque/synagogue?
18. Are there other people of my nationality living nearby with whom I could make friends?
19. Is the area considered a 'safe' neighbourhood? Have there been reports of attacks/burglaries/rapes/vandalism? (If there are, your landlord won't tell you. Chat to the neighbours.)
20. Is this an upper class/middle class/working class area?
21. Is there space for my car?
22. Is there somewhere to put my bicycle?
23. Does the place look clean, does everything appear to be in good working order?
24. Can I have pets?

Accommodation to let

Professional woman wanted to share flat, centre Oakhurst, all amenities, £50 per week inc. parking. Phone Sue on 00000/00000 after 6pm.

Well-furnished, self-contained bedsit on small farm between Oakhurst and Greenenden. Tel. 00000/00000.

Centrally heated ground floor flat, suit couple and child, furnished and close to town centre. No pets. £75 p/w. Available March. Tel. 00000/00000.

Oakhurst, close to railway station. Very pleasant 2nd floor studio flat. Newly decorated, new carpets, telephone point. Rent £195 per calendar month. Phone Oakhurst 00000/00000.

Flatshare: room available near Oakhurst Green Square. Non-smoker only. Tel. 00000/00000. (day time).

Two-bedroomed unfurnished cottage, £95pw, deposit and references required. Tel. 00000/00000.

Terraced house, three bedrooms, lounge, dining room, large fitted kitchen, central heating, part double glazed, fitted carpets. Oakhurst town centre area. £110pw. 00000/00000.

3 bed garden flat £100 per week near Oakhurst. Deposit required. 00000/00000.

A room to let in house share. Full use of all facilities. Non-smoker. No bills. £40pw. 00000/00000.

Oakhurst town: 2-bed, spacious maisonette, quiet area, available immediately, suit elderly retired person or couple. Please phone 00000/00000.

To share: 2-bedroomed spacious flat, share with one other female Tel.00000/00000.

Fig. 6. Sample 'accommodation to let' advertisements.

GETTING HELP

Contact the following organisations for advice, especially on finding student accommodation:

British Council Arrivals Unit, 10 Spring Gardens, London WW1A 2BN (London area).

British Tourist Authority, 12 Regent Street, London SW1Y 4PQ (hotel accommodation).

Experiment in International Living, 'Otesaga', West Malvern Road, Malvern, Worcestershire WR14 4EN (homestays with British families).

HOST, 18 Northumberland Avenue, London WC2N 5BJ (homestays with British families).

International Students House, 229 Great Portland Street, London WIN 5HD.

London Hostels Association, 54 Eccleston Square, London SW1V 1PG (student hostels).

Piccadilly Advice Centre, 100 Shaftsbury Avenue, London W1V 7DH (information on hostels).

Student Accommodation Service, 67 Wigmore Street, London W1H 9LG (London area).

Women's Link, la Snow Hill Court, London EC1A 2EJ (accommodation for women in London).

Young Men's Christian Association, 640 Forest Road, London E17 3DZ.

Young Women's Christian Association, 16 Great Russell Street, London WC1B 3LR.

Youth Hostels Association, Trevelyan House, 8 St Stephen's Hill, St Albans, Hertfordshire AL1 2DY (temporary accommodation).

A useful leaflet is *Address list for international students*, published by UKCOSA (see Useful Addresses).

BUYING HOUSEHOLD ITEMS

The British taste in decorating and furnishing may differ from yours. They like to combine many different patterns: wallpaper, curtains, cushions, upholstery, carpets, everything comes in patterns. It is considered good style to combine flowers, stripes and tartans, as long as there is an overall theme, such as 'cottage garden'.

There are several magazines dedicated solely to interior decoration. Choosing the colour schemes, patterns and furniture is usually the privilege of the lady of the house. The man may occasionally get asked what he likes, but she tends to get on with her plans regardless of his tastes. After all, she knows what's fashionable and he does not.

There are furniture shops in all medium and large towns. It's cheaper if you assemble the items yourself. Shops specialising in self-assembly furniture include Focus Do It All and MFI.

Household equipment can be bought in high street and specialist shops. You can also buy saucepans, spoons, tea towels and so on in discount shops. The products bought there are not always of good quality but are probably fine if you plan to stay only for a year or so.

Charity shops sell household items second hand, but unlike clothes, they don't provide real savings. However, car boot sales can be excellent sources for cheap second hand household items.

If you don't have the time to go out shopping, consider buying self-assembly furniture from a mail order catalogue. Furniture is slightly more expensive by mail order than from Focus Do It All or MFI, but it saves you the trouble of transporting the items home. Mail order catalogues also sell household items.

CASE STUDIES

Hanna moves around
'I moved seven or eight times in the first year because I could not find what I wanted. Now I've found myself a nice flat and am happy.'

Deborah appreciates the contact
'When I first arrived from the US, I found myself a place in a flatshare. I'm glad I did this, and I would recommend it to anyone who is new to the country. It is so useful if there is always someone around whom you can ask for information and advice.'

Helmut rejects the champagne glasses
'My wife and I were viewing a one-bedroom flat to rent for a year. The agent had described it as "fully furnished". There was no wardrobe, no cupboard, no fridge, no table, no chairs. All there was was a bed, six whisky tumblers, 24 champagne flutes, and five china ducks.

'What sort of life did they expect us to lead in the flat? We complained to the agent who acted surprised: "We consider this

fully furnished. We reckon you could live with that. And aren't the china ducks a nice touch?"
'We did not think so and declined.'

Claudia's landlord spies at the door

'I am a temporary secretary, and I'm moving around a lot, wherever the job is. The places in the "stockbroker belt" within commuting distance of London were the worst.

'I had one landlady attack me with her fingernails because she did not approve of my hoovering method. One landlord followed me upstairs every night and spent about two hours just standing outside my door. He never came in, but it was unnerving. A couple with whom I shared a flat invited me to watch them have sex in the lounge.

'One landlady kept rummaging through my drawers in my absence. Another one accused me in front of neighbours of having male visitors for immoral purposes. The only male visitor I had received in the place was a young man who brought me a flower and a card for my birthday and stayed for coffee.

'Another used to have servants, but could not afford them any more. For a while she had an au pair, but even that got too expensive. So she took in lodgers who lived in the former servants' rooms and paid her instead of demanding wages. Unfortunately she could not adjust mentally to the new situation. She treated us like servants, shouted at us, demanded that we bow and curtsey, and interfered with our lives.

'Remarkably, I never had any problems with flatmates or landladies in London. I think in London people are more used to sharing accommodation or to having lodgers.'

Michael learns about the housing market

'I met a couple who owned a two bedroomed house. They wanted to sell their home and buy a four bedroomed house in the neighbour-hood instead. They told me they were just waiting for house prices to go up again, so that they could sell their house at a profit, and thus afford the four bedroomed house.

'Now I didn't know much about the British housing market, but common sense told me that there was a flaw in their plan. I asked them if they didn't think that the four bedroomed house would go up in price as well.

' "No, that could not happen. We want to buy it at the price it is now. We just want more money for our present house." '

'They were highly intelligent and educated people, both graduates. But when the house prices finally went up in that area, the owners of the four-bedroomed house asked for a higher price too. The couple complained to me that they were being cheated. They were outraged and called it unfair.'

Lynne notes house selling practices
'If you're buying a house here, be aware of the system of blind bidding which is in common use. Also watch out for the practice of 'gazumping' and 'gazundering' (I'm not making these words up), which means that a property may be sold out from under you at the last minute, even when you think you have it signed for. You can't be sure that the property transfer is complete until you have the keys in your hand.'

POINTS TO CONSIDER

1. What is more important for you: the flexibility of renting, which allows you to change accommodation or move to another area without committing a large sum of money, or the feeling of having your own place, independence and privacy?

2. How long do you plan to stay in Britain? Would it be a good move to buy rather than rent accommodation?

3. If you plan to buy property and take out a mortgage: what happens if you lose your job, if you have to move to another part of the country, or if you decide to return to your home country?

4. If you plan to settle in the UK with your family and think of buying a home: how will your requirements change over the next few years? For example, will you want to be near playgrounds or near schools?

9

Going to Work

There are no statutory regulations in the UK concerning maximum working hours. You will find a wide variation in working practices throughout the country. Most workers work a 37.5 hour working week, with four weeks (20 working days) annual holiday. If there is a lot of work to be done, your employers will expect you to work overtime. Some employers pay for overtime, others assume that it is included in your regular payment, some will give you time off in lieu.

When people are afraid of losing their jobs, they will put in a lot of extra (unpaid) hours, just to impress their boss with their industry, even if they are not asked to. Research shows that the increased work hours don't result in higher productivity or better quality.

Trade unions have lost much of their power, and employers are not obliged to recognise them for negotiation and representations. But they still exist and they negotiate on behalf of the workforce in many industries. Ask your colleagues whether it would be useful for you to join a trade union.

SIGNING YOUR CONTRACT

When you are offered a contract, check the terms and conditions carefully. Make sure you understand fully what you are signing.

Contracts can vary in length from one paragraph to several pages. Contracts often come in the form of a letter from your employer or head of department, outlining the job offer, and asking you to countersign the letter or write a letter of confirmation (see Figure 10).

If you have not received a contract by the time you start working, keep asking until you get one.

This does not apply to temp jobs for which employers rarely offer contracts. But even for temp jobs, you may ask for a brief letter confirming the arrangements.

The International PR Company

Ms Sabine Schmidt
2 Wax Road
Slushton, AB1 2CD

1 March 200X

Dear Sabine,

We agreed that you will be starting as our new bilingual
secretary/PA on 1 April, in our Oakhurst office. Your work
hours will be Monday-Friday 9am-5pm, with 20 days annual
holiday entitlement.

You will be reporting to our managing director, Ms Eve
Pankhurst. Your duties will include taking dictation, typing,
filing, translating, wordprocessing, organising Ms
Pankhurst's diary, and liaising with clients on the phone.

We look forward to welcoming you on 1 April. In the
meantime, please don't hesitate to phone if you have any
questions.

Yours sincerely

Cynthia
Cynthia Clare (Ms)
Personnel Manager

Fig. 7. Sample work contract.

Remember that if you work in the UK, the employment legislation in your home country no longer protects you. The conditions of employment are a matter of agreement between you and your employer, and subject only to UK legislation.

Checklist: your work contract
Your contract should contain the following points:

● your job title

● a brief job description

● the person you are reporting to (your immediate boss)

● your place of work

● your work hours (how many hours per week, which days, which hours)

● how much you will earn

● how often, when and how you will be paid

● your annual holiday entitlement

● when and how the contract can be terminated.

Getting paid
Most workers and employees get paid monthly, either by cheque or directly into their bank account. Remember to sort out a **bank account** before the first payment arrives. If you don't have a bank account yet, let the personnel or accounts department know – they may be able to give you your first payment in cash.

You will usually get your payment towards the end of the working month. The sum you receive will already have the income tax and national insurance (and, if appropriate, your contributions to a company pension scheme) deducted.

Seasonal workers – such as fruit pickers – are sometimes paid in cash on a weekly or daily basis, or by bucket or bin.

When you are negotiating your payment, you and your employer will talk about annual full-time earnings (p.a. = per annum), even if you are working only part-time on a job share, or if you are on a six-month contract.

Equal opportunities

British people, especially in London, are used to working side by side with foreigners, so you are unlikely to be discriminated against in your daily work because of your nationality. But in getting a job and in gaining promotion your origins may prove a handicap.

Racial and sexual discrimination are unlawful. Women in Britain are entitled to equal pay with men, when doing similar work. This sounds great in theory, but in practice women often don't get the top jobs even if they are just as qualified as male candidates. The same applies to people of ethnic origin.

It is difficult to prove that you are being discriminated against because of your gender or race. If you are certain, you could take legal advice on which steps to take. Talk to your trade union representative initially or visit your nearest Citizens Advice Bureau.

On the whole, the situation for women and coloured people is improving rapidly. You can find some women and people from various ethnic origins in middle management positions, and a few in top management. You can probably achieve the same as a white Anglo-Saxon male – but you will have to work much harder for it and be much better at your job than your male white colleagues.

The rise of ageism

One form of discrimination is widespread in the UK and not unlawful. This is ageism. Many job applicants find they are not being considered for a job if they are older than 40. People who are already working for a company find they are not getting promoted because they have reached 40. This is of course ridiculous – a mature applicant is probably just as flexible and healthy as a young candidate, has almost certainly more experience and probably more loyalty. But personnel managers like to think in categories, and 'jobs vacant' adverts ask for applications from 'suitably qualified candidates aged 25–40'.

GETTING ON WITH YOUR COLLEAGUES

People who work together don't normally spend their spare time together, although there will probably be the occasional department party or company Christmas lunch.

It is OK to invite colleagues from your department to a meal or for drinks in your home, but don't be disappointed if they don't accept the invitation. Some people strongly believe in keeping work and private life separate. However, it's worth trying, especially if you are new to the country, have few friends, and your colleagues are the only people you know.

If a colleague is leaving, your department will probably collect money for a farewell gift (around £1 from each colleague), and maybe take the person to the pub for drinks, or the person leaving will bring a bottle of wine on the last day.

Birthdays are not usually celebrated, but this depends on the company. In many companies it is customary to give a Christmas card to everyone working in your department, as well as to everyone in other departments with whom you work closely.

Bringing in a treat

You can occasionally bring a bar of chocolate or another sweet (if possible made in your home country) and give everyone in your department a piece. 'I've brought some Swiss chocolate/Chinese peanuts – would you like some?'

This helps break the ice and make the day more pleasant. It's also a good opening for a little chat. Don't choose anything expensive, or they will feel obliged to reciprocate. Avoid alcohol unless it's a special occasion and your boss gives permission.

There will probably be a coffee machine or coffee making facilities. British people like drinking hot tea or coffee when they are at work. For some machines, you have to insert coins. Sometimes everyone pays a specific amount into a communal box – for example, 20 pence per cup or £4 per month.

When you arrive in the office, and the first time you see a person that day, greet them with 'Good morning'. If you leave for your lunch break, say 'See you later' to the people in the same room. When you leave for the day, say 'Good night', even if it is only late afternoon.

CASE STUDIES

Claudia has to fight for her money

'My first job as a secretary was awful. To start with, there wasn't any work to do. I existed just as a status symbol for my boss. One partner in the firm had a French bilingual secretary, so the other partner wanted an Italian bilingual secretary. Most of the time we were just sitting around doing crosswords. Occasionally we had to write a letter, or were asked to type memos. This company had a real memo culture. Secretaries typed memos to other secretaries to confirm they had received a previous memo to their boss.

'I was meant to be paid weekly, but whenever I asked for my money, they had a different excuse: they couldn't find the cheque book, or the person who signed salary cheques was on holiday. I stayed for seven weeks. Towards the end of this period I lived on bread without butter, half an apple and one tomato each day. The company was so mean with money, but supplied free coffee. I drank lots of coffee with four lumps of sugar in each cup and plenty of milk. I was down to my last ten pounds. I knew I could not even afford to buy a weekly Underground travelcard for next week, or enough food to live on.

'Luckily, I received a phone call from an employment agency with whom I had registered and then de-registered after finding the job. The consultant asked me if I was happy, and when I said no, she said she might have a job for me: marketing secretary for a company which planned to export to Italy. I got the job on the spot, with a proper contract. Mind you, I still had to survive the first month until I got my first salary – a friend lent me some luncheon vouchers and my landlady agreed to wait for my rent. All in all, my first weeks were horrible.'

Deborah adjusts to work attitudes

'British work attitudes are different to the United States. People here are very cautious, and reluctant to put themselves forward. I worked in computer marketing and I found this attitude frustrating, because little gets done. They are so careful not to cause offence, and they will not talk about difficulties and differences as openly as the Americans do.'

POINTS TO CONSIDER

1. Do you know any nationals of your country who have worked in Britain? What were their experiences? How did they perceive British work attitudes?

2. Are you willing to work overtime? How much? For how long? If you feel your employers are exploiting you, how are you going to express your protest politely?

3. What will you do if you encounter open or hidden hostilities

from your colleagues, on grounds of your ethnic origin or nationality?

4. What will you do if you don't get on with your colleagues or your boss?

5. Imagine the worst possible scenario – whatever would make working life really difficult or unpleasant to you. Imagine how it would make you feel, then think about how you would respond to solve the problem or get out of the situation.

10

Living in Britain

SHOPPING

Most shops are open Mondays to Saturdays from 9am to 5 or 5.30pm, but there are exceptions (for example, late-night shopping and Sunday opening, especially in the superstores). If there are several people in the shop waiting to be served, you have to form a queue.

Specialist shops versus superstores

Britain used to be renowned for its small specialist shops. But the **grocers**, **butchers**, **bakers** and **ironmongers** are disappearing in many towns. **Supermarkets** (which sell all types of foodstuffs) and **superstores** (which sell many other items besides) attract the customers.

It cannot be said that one is cheaper than the other. Supermarkets often sell a few important items cheaper than the shops to attract customers, but make up for it with much higher prices for other goods.

Shopping in superstores has the advantage that you can do all your purchases in one shop, and you need to find a car parking space only once. However, the small specialist shops almost always offer more specialist knowledge and competent advice.

There are some specialist shops which you may not have in your home country. For example, the **sweet shops**. These sell cigarettes, chocolates *etc* and are open on Sundays and late in the evenings. This is because it is considered essential that everyone has the opportunity to buy cigarettes and sweets should they need them suddenly (more important than the availability of milk or bread, for example). The British won't understand why you find this strange. Sometimes sweet shops are combined with newsagents.

Card shops sell nothing but birthday cards, Christmas cards, gift wrapping paper and balloons.

You will notice that many shops in British shopping areas (usually referred to as **high streets**) are empty, often with the shopfronts boarded up, disfigured with graffiti or smashed windows. These shops had to close down due to the difficult economic climate and the competition from superstores. As soon as some shops in a road are closed, customers don't enjoy shopping there any more, the remaining shops close too, and the road is doomed. This can be a depressing sight.

Village and corner shops

Many **village shops** face the same fate. More and more village people work in towns and do their shopping on the way home at a supermarket, or go on weekly shopping trips to the nearest superstore. It's worth patronising the village shops, however. They have a surprisingly large range of goods for sale, and often at very reasonable prices. Some of them achieve this by joining a cooperative with other small shops, thus buying larger quantities from the wholesalers and getting a better deal.

Think what a loss it would be if your village lost its shop – especially if you are ill, if the village gets snowed in, or if something else happens and you can't leave the village. Corner shops have a similar function, but in towns and cities. They are surprisingly often owned and managed by Indian or Pakistani people, and they compete with the superstores by offering opening hours which are convenient for working people: until late in the evening, and on Sundays, for example.

Discount shops are also a feature of British high streets. Here, you can buy many items at a reduced price. Some are end-of-the-range goods, some are seconds (that is, goods which have a tiny fault), others are made from cheaper materials than usual.

Farmers' markets are a new trend. Many British people are fed up with buying fruit and vegetables in supermarkets, where the produce looks good, but seldom has much flavour. Apples coming from as far as New Zealand or the USA contribute to the traffic and pollution problems, while a variety of exciting-tasting apples from local farmers are not considered by the supermarkets because they are not grown in large enough quantities. So local farmers get together and hold their own local weekly markets where local people can buy fresh local produce. You'll probably find hen's, duck's and goose eggs, cheeses made from cow's, sheep and goat's milk, wines, home-made jams and jellies. Depending on the season, a vast variety of fragrant apples, pears, apricots, cherries, strawberries, gooseberries, raspberries and currants, as well as vegetables such as potatoes, leeks, marrows, carrots and onions.

Another way to get really fresh fruit is to **pick your own**. Many farms offer this option. Instead of paying harvest workers and storing the produce, they allow you to go directly into the fields and orchards and pick your own straight from the plant. The apples, strawberries, redcurrants or raspberries are wonderfully fresh and cheap, and you get exercise in the fresh air. Watch out for signs saying 'Pick Your Own' (PYO for short).

Another place where you can do your shopping cheaply is the **street markets**. Many towns have a market every week. You will probably pay only 60 per cent of the supermarket prices for fruit and vegetables. Clothes and household items are similar to discount shops.

Mail order

You can get mail order **catalogues**, especially for clothing, but also for household items and furniture. Mail order shopping has the advantage that you need not leave the house to do your shopping.

If something doesn't fit or look right, you can return it for a refund. Items will be delivered to and collected from your doorstep free of charge. Occasionally, there is trouble when the mail order company claims that you have not returned your goods, when urgently needed orders don't arrive and so on. This can be so annoying that it puts some people off mail order altogether.

Mail order shopping is slightly more expensive (but not much more) than high street shopping.

You will find addresses of some mail order companies in the Useful Addresses.

COMPLAINING

Most British shops are very good at accepting complaints. If an item is faulty, and sometimes even if you have simply changed your mind, they will exchange the item for another one or refund your money. You will be asked to show your receipt.

If you feel that you have been cheated by a shop – maybe the quality of the goods wasn't as promised – and the shop refuses to put matters right, you can report them to the **Trading Standards Office**. Simply phone or write. You'll find the address in the phone book, either under Trading Standards or under the county council's list of numbers.

Don't be shy or apologetic: they welcome your comments, and if the shop is in the wrong, the officers will see to it that matters are put right.

BUYING SECOND HAND

Charity shops

Charity shops, almost unknown in other parts of the world, are popular in Britain. They sell second-hand items, mostly clothing, and the proceeds go to a charity. People donate clothes they have outgrown and unwanted Christmas presents to the shop.

Charity shops are fantastic places to shop if you need clothes suitable for British life, but don't have enough money to buy a complete new wardrobe. I found a pair of leather shoes, almost new (£1), a designer ballgown for a special occasion (£20), a pair of jeans (£3), a summer dress (£1.50) and a good quality suit (£4.50), all in favourite colours and perfect fits.

However, it's a matter of luck. You may find something you like, but it's in the wrong size. Some charity shops also sell household items and furniture. You'll notice that some charity shops are better kept than others. If a charity shop looks and smells dirty, don't shop there.

Boot fairs

Car boot fairs take place at weekends in spring, summer and autumn, usually on sports grounds or fields. Almost every village has at least one boot fair per year. People put up stalls to sell items they no longer want or need. You as the customer pay about 20 pence admission, and then you can buy cheaply whatever you fancy. It's alright to bargain for the price. Occasionally there are commercial traders as well; they charge higher prices. It's a matter of luck if you find what you want. If you enjoy visiting several boot fairs each week, you will have almost everything you could possibly need at the end of the season.

This year, I bought the following: a light box for transparencies (£1 – new it would have cost about £100), a pair of brand new leather sandals (£5 – sold in shops at £40), a pair of jeans (£1), a slide projector stand (£1.50), a warm winter jacket (£2), about 100 books (between 5p and £1 each), a beautiful knitted cardigan (£4), file cards (£1 – would have cost about £6 new) and much more.

Boot fairs are excellent places for buying children's clothes. If you want to find really good items, you must get up early and go there at about 7am. On the other hand, the best bargains can be had just before the boot fair closes, at about 12 noon when the vendors pack up and sell everything for pennies.

Jumble sales

Jumble sales take place in village or church halls, usually on Saturday afternoons in autumn and winter. Start queuing outside about a quarter of an hour before the official start. You pay about 20 pence admission, and then you can buy any item for 10 or 20 pence.

You will find mostly clothing, piled up on tables. There may also be books and household items. Think in advance what items you want, what your family's sizes and favourite colours are. If you see something, grab it. Don't think twice, or it will be gone. There won't be the time to check for stains or damages.

Just pick 10 or 20 items, pay for them, and discard afterwards what you don't want.

At a recent jumble sale, I spent £1.50 (including admission). After throwing out a skirt that didn't fit and a tracksuit with stains, I was left with: two jerseys, three blouses, a pair of baggy summer trousers, a summer dress, a wool scarf and two T-shirts. New, the items would have cost over £100.

Barter trade

Over recent years, LETS (Local Exchange Barter Systems) have taken hold. These allow you to get everything you want without paying money. Members try to go back to a time before there was money, and swap goods and services, but with an extra twist: you don't have to do direct swaps. Instead, you can render a service to one member of the group and receive a service from another.

These groups are usually run by volunteers, and how well they work depends on the enthusiasm of the members and the efficiency of the people who lead them. It takes a lot of work to keep a group going, keeping accounts of who has given or taken how much.

I belong to several LETS barter groups. I have received the following without payment: haircuts, a carpenter repairing our garden bench and greenhouse, an artist illustrating one of my books, another artist painting a mural on my office wall, yet another artist to paint local miniatures, cut flower arrangements for the guest artists who performed in my shows, handmade candles, a box of freshly harvested apples, hand-made jewellery, poetry and much more.

In return, I have given private lessons in journalism and

bellydance, entertained as a bellydancer at parties, edited a newsletter, given tarot readings. I have traded herb plants and flowers from my greenhouse, the clothes from the days when I was a size 12, clutter from the attic and more.

The nicest thing about barter trade is that you can offer to do things you really enjoy doing. Whatever your skills and interests are, you can offer them: translations from or into your own language, or teaching it, dressmaking, embroidery, writing poetry, typing, filing, house cleaning, entertaining at children's parties, childminding, plumbing, ironing, dog walking. However esoteric your offers, someone may need just that. Perhaps you can impersonate Tony Blair or teach a parrot how to speak? If you have a lot of clutter and not much space, you can dispose of some of your stuff this way.

In return, you could ask for English lessons, someone to edit your CV, household items, plants for your new garden, someone to help you redecorate the flat, and anything else you need. If your group is efficient, you will be able to find much – but probably not all – you want without paying money for it. You'll probably have to pay for the materials (e.g. the paint) in cash, and some groups allow members to charge for their services partly in money.

How to be an effective LETS member:

- Don't try to 'save up' credits – start 'spending' as soon as you join. LETS credits are not like money, and the system works only if people spend.

- Offer as many services as you can think of, even if you can't believe that anyone would want them. But offer only what you are willing to do.

- If a job is important, check the service provider's credentials. For example, don't let strangers look after your children without asking for references, and don't let an electrician rewire your house without checking their qualifications.

To find out about local LETS or other barter system groups in your area, ask your borough council, parish council or library.

CHOOSING NEWSPAPERS AND MAGAZINES

You will find that there are newspapers or magazines for almost every area of work and leisure (from *Darts Player* to *Racing Pigeon Pictorial*, from *Design and Technology Teaching* to *Commercial*

Motor). There are also many general interest magazines, most of them aimed at women. The choice can be bewildering, but each magazine is aimed at a specific type of person (age group, marital status, level of education) and you will soon find out which suits you best.

For general interest and some hobby magazines, go to your local **newsagents**. Newsagents will also order and arrange regular delivery of daily newspapers for you. The more specialised publications are delivered by post. You have to take out an annual subscription.

EATING

Most British people take the main meal of the day in the evening. It's called **dinner** or **supper**. If they are in a hurry, they will make beans on toast. Recipe: Open a can of baked beans, put them in a saucepan and heat. Put two slices of bread into a toaster. Put bread on plate and beans on bread.

For **lunch** (the midday meal), they usually have sandwiches. You can buy sandwiches from many shops. A sandwich consists of slices of bread with salad, meat, fish or cheese. You may find it confusing that menus and price lists just drop the word 'sandwich'. For example, 'tuna salad' is not a salad at all, but a sandwich filled with tuna, a lettuce leaf, a couple of tomato slices and three or four cucumber slices.

Very few British people now take the time to prepare the once traditional cooked **breakfast** of hot sausages, eggs, bacon or ham. Most prefer a quick slice of toast, or a bowl of cereal with milk.

Restaurants
You can eat simple but hearty meals at low prices in **pubs**, but only at specified times. **Restaurants** are more expensive and have a larger menu. Many restaurants offer foreign cuisine. Indian and Chinese meals are particularly popular (although Indian and Chinese people are sometimes surprised how the dishes have been adapted to suit British tastebuds).

In most restaurants you wait near the entrance until staff lead you to a table.

Fast food and take-aways
The British like take-away food. It's less work than home cooking, but cheaper than eating out.

Pizzas
These can be ordered by telephone – someone will deliver the pizzas to your home by motorbike or car.

Fast food
Fast food restaurants sell hamburgers *etc* to eat in or to eat out. They are the same all over the world and you are probably familiar with them.

Fish and chips
This is the traditional British take-away. In its original form, the deep-fried battered fish fillet and the chips were wrapped in newspapers. Nowadays many shops use plastic containers which are not environmentally friendly but keep the food warm for longer. The bigger fish and chip shops offer a choice of fish varieties. Cod is the cheapest and most popular. Fish and chips is a healthy meal, providing carbohydrates, protein and vitamins, but unfortunately has an excess of fat, which makes it unsuitable for an everyday diet.

Jacket potatoes
Also known as potatoes in their jackets, baked potatoes, or spuds. Large potatoes, baked in the oven, then halved and filled with butter or cheese or baked beans. Many other fillings may also be available. A healthy take-away/fast food option, although sometimes the potatoes have been baked for so long and re-heated so often that most of the vitamins are destroyed.

Chinese
Chinese take-way food is relatively rich in vitamins and low in fat. It tends to be expensive. If you buy one portion of vegetables and one portion of rice you will probably have enough for two people.

ENJOYING YOUR HOBBIES AND LEISURE

Coffee mornings
Coffee mornings are an important part of British rural life. Most coffee mornings take place mid-week. Some are by invitation only, others are open to the public. For some, there is an admission fee and the coffee is free; others give free admission but charge for the coffee. The money goes to a charity.

To raise more money for the charity, there will also be a raffle.

you buy a strip of tickets which costs 50p or £1. Never buy just one ticket or you will be considered mean. At the end of the coffee morning, the first raffle winner can choose an item from the prize selection. The second winner has second choice and so on, until all prizes are gone.

There may also be a bring and buy. Everyone donates something: an unwanted Christmas present, second hand items in good condition, home-made jam or jelly, or a home-baked cake. Everyone buys something, and the money goes to charity.

Expect to spend about £2.50 on admission, coffee, raffle and bring and buy.

Joining groups, clubs and societies

Your first time in Britain can be a period of isolation and loneliness. You are not supposed to talk to people unless you have been introduced to them. The quickest way of getting introductions is to join a group, club or society. As soon as you are a member, you are considered 'introduced' to every other member and can make contact.

In small towns, you will find Townswomen's Guilds and local history societies. Towns and cities also have many hobby and special interest groups: diving clubs, writers' circles, photography clubs and so on.

The typical set-up in a village would be: bingo club, Women's Institute (monthly lectures and activities), horticultural society (lots of competitions for the most perfect rose or the largest cucumber), amateur dramatics society, footpath group (walks in and around the village). Most of them meet once a month.

To find out which hobby groups and societies are active in your town or village, ask at the local library. They will probably have a file of groups and contacts.

British-international societies

If you find it difficult to meet British people, or if the different customs, attitudes and mentality sometimes nearly drive you mad, try to make friends among expatriates. It's good to talk to someone who is in the same boat. There are many Anglo-international friendship societies in Britain, most of them based in London. By joining them, you can meet fellow expats as well as Britons with a strong interest in your home country. You will find many addresses in the Useful Addresses section, or you can contact your embassy or high commission.

HAVING FUN ON A BUDGET

There are many ways of spending money on leisure. You will soon find out which are the most pleasant ways for you, and won't need advice. It's different if you want to enjoy yourself but money is tight. Here are a few suggestions:

- Go to the **museum**. Some museums charge no admission fee, including the National Gallery and the National Portrait Gallery in London.

- Join the **library**. Once you have registered, you can borrow several books each month, free of charge.

- Go on **footpath walks**. There are monthly walks, usually on Sunday afternoons, in and around most villages. They last about two hours and are guided, and there is seldom a charge.

- Watch **amateur theatre performances**. They are not free, but tickets cost far less than for professional performances. You will be surprised how high the standards are. There are many amateur dramatic societies, so there will certainly be a show in your area.

PRACTISING YOUR RELIGION

The national religion is Christianity which comes with a confusing number of sub-groups: from 'high church' (with emphasis on ritual) to 'low church' (which is more informal), Quakers, Methodists, Baptists, Roman Catholics and so on. Many English people refer to their religion as 'CofE' (Church of England, a term which embraces a variety of Christian groups).

It is a matter of 'shopping around' to see which form of worship and attitude suits you best, or is similar to the way you worship in your home country.

In London some Christian churches hold services according to the customs and in the languages of other countries.

The British are, on the whole, tolerant about other religions. They will not stop you from practising your religion, but may be annoyed if you try to convert them.

Every large town has a mosque and a synagogue. The cities also have places of worship for other religions.

Paganism is a fast growing religion in the UK, especially among the young. Most pagans follow either the Wiccan or the Druid paths, but there are also goddess Worshippers, Shamans and Odinists.

While many Britons are demonstrative about their religion by displaying a symbol of their faith – Christians for example like wearing a pendant in the shape of a cross or a fish, or put a fish logo in their business advertisements – others prefer to keep their faith private and remain quiet about it. That's why there are no reliable statistics about who believes in what. A commonly used statistic says there are roughly 27 million Anglicans, 9 million Roman Catholics, 1 million Muslims, 800,000 Presbyterians, 760,000 Methodists, 400,000 Sikhs, 350,000 Hindus and 300,000 Jews.

Most religions do not have central headquarters, but here are some addresses which may serve as a starting point for finding a community of your faith. Some of these organisations are operating on a small budget and would appreciate a stamped addressed envelope or international reply coupon. You can also ask at your borough council's information office or at the local library.

CHECKLIST

1. Which shops are near where I live? What can I buy there?

2. Where is the nearest supermarket? How do I get there?

3. Have I made lists of furniture, household equipment and clothes I want to buy?

4. Which of these items could I possibly buy second hand?

5. Have I obtained a mail order catalogue?

6. Where is the nearest group of people who share my hobby?

7. Have I joined the library?

8. Which groups, clubs and societies meet near where I live?

9. Where is the nearest place of worship for my religion?

CASE STUDIES

Hanna buys a gift

'During my first week in London, I bought a small vase as a gift. I automatically asked the sales assistant: "Can you wrap it up as a gift, please?" Giftwrapping is a service which shops in the

Netherlands provide for free. But the London sales assistant nearly dropped the vase. Her mouth was gaping open in astonishment, and she said: "Madam, we do not wrap gifts! You have to go to a card shop down the road and buy gift wrapping paper and ribbon and do it yourself."

'So I went and bought some wrapping material, which cost almost as much as the gift itself.'

Mehmet finds the British helpful

'On my first day at the language school, the tutor said: "You are from Turkey. I wonder if you are a Muslim? We have not had Muslims before, so I don't know what you need, but I've prepared this for you." She gave me a sheet of paper which contained not only the address of the local mosque and of an Islamic society, but also instructions how to get there.

'Later, I was invited to a party at a British friend's home. He didn't know much about Islam, but asked: "Is there anything we should know? Anything you don't eat, or anything we must not do in your presence? We would not want to offend you in your religion. Please forgive us if we offend you by mistake." I find the British very ignorant about Islam, but they try to be tolerant.'

Mansour observes different manners

'The British are so correct in many ways, but they do things which would be extremely rude in Iran. For example, they blow their noses in the presence of other people. The first time I saw and heard someone blow their nose in a crowded underground train, I couldn't stop laughing. It seemed so rude and uncivilised, and so funny.'

Pierre complains to Trading Standards

'In February, I was shopping in a supermarket. They had a promotional sign up: "French apples, freshly harvested". Every single crate of French apples was labelled "New harvest". I asked to speak to the produce manager, and asked him where in France they were harvesting apples in February. He told me that "new harvest" referred to the apples being taken freshly out of cold store. I requested him to remove the sign, and he refused.

'I phoned the Trading Standards office who agreed that the signs were misleading the consumers and thanked me for informing them. Two days later, I visited the supermarket again. The "new harvest" signs had disappeared.'

Lynne likes the safety of Scotland

'I feel Aberdeen is a much safer city to live in than just about any city in the US. I can walk down the street at 1am without being afraid of an attack, although the level of violence has increased since I first moved here. I like the pubs and the social scene. People here take the time to go out and just talk, hang out with each other, even when they are working adults. I feel this is something that a lot of people in America have forgotten how to do. On the whole, I find the pubs here much nicer places than bars in America.

'Housing is cheaper in Scotland than in the USA. Clothing is a lot more expensive, don't buy it here if you can help it – except wool sweaters or 'jumpers', since Scotland produces a lot of them. Food is generally a bit more expensive here, although staples like milk and bread are actually cheaper.

'It is no coincidence that Scotland has the highest rate of heart disease of any European country. Most things are still cooked in fat. There are places in Aberdeen and Glasgow that sell, I kid you not, deep-fat fried pizzas and deep-fat fried Mars bars. Chips (proper, thick French fries that is) and crisps (potato chips) are still a staple of the average diet. Fish and Chips shops are everywhere, and you can just stand there and listen to your arteries hardening. You can get crisps in flavours you would never have thought to stick in a potato chip: roast beef, ham and mustard, prawn. Fresh fruit and veggies are a lot more expensive than in America and the variety is limited.'

Fiona tries country and city life

'I'm a country girl and have been my whole life. When I first came to the UK I lived on an estate in the Scottish countryside. I started hunting, which was great, and I went shooting. But now I am in London, and the difference is huge. Here I am living in one of the biggest cities and having a great time. Of course there's no hunting or shooting here, and my whole lifestyle has changed. I miss my Scottish friends. Here in London I'm socialising mostly with other Australians and Kiwis, and we all have a ball.'

Sigal runs out of money

'The most difficult thing about living in London is the money. I never have enough of it, and that makes everything else so much more difficult. Seeing homeless people everywhere all the time gets me down – you simply don't see that in Australia. Overall I have become a very different person to who I was in Australia. I went from being an 18-year-old sheltered girl to someone who throws herself into life in London's diverse culture. My advice to other Australians who want to come to London is, don't expect life here to be cheap. Even if you save up money at home, you will lose it all in two weeks because the pound is so strong. When you come here, find work as soon as possible.'

Zinga finds many mosques
'It is easy for muslims to practise their faith here in England, because there are a lot of mosques.'

POINTS TO CONSIDER

1. Do you want to practise your religion in Britain?

2. If there is no place of worship where you live, are you prepared to travel to other towns, or would you consider joining the worship of another religious group?

3. If you take your family, will there be schools which educate your child in your religious beliefs? If not, would your child benefit from religious instruction in Christian beliefs?

11

Understanding Holidays and Traditions

CELEBRATING CHRISTMAS

Christmas takes place on 25 December to celebrate what is supposed to be Jesus Christ's birthday. But the preparations begin as early as July, when you will get the first mail order Christmas catalogues. In October the shops start putting up Christmas decorations.

Mistletoe twigs hang in door frames, and if you stand under one, you may be kissed. There are lots of fir branches (real and plastic), colourful paper garlands, candles (mostly electric), Christmas trees (real or artificial), singing and jokes. Christmas is also a traditional time for having an argument with your partner, parents, children and in-laws and for people deciding to get divorced or to commit suicide.

Most British people send or give Christmas cards to all friends, neighbours and colleagues. The average Briton sends about 100 cards every year. This can be expensive, especially if you add up the postage. Received Christmas cards are displayed around the fireplace and on bookshelves, or hung on strings along the walls.

If you want to follow the custom, buy the cheapest pack of 50 or so cards. Don't worry about whether or not a card is beautiful. There is no accounting for British taste. If you spend a lot of money on really special cards, chances are that the recipient won't notice the special effort because she gets so many cards, and she may not like what you find beautiful anyway. Deliver as many cards by hand as you possibly can to save on postage.

Christmas crackers are those long things where you and your table neighbours hold one end each and pull. It makes a bang of varying loudness and the one who holds the longer end wins the prize (usually some silly plastic finger ring or plastic car model, worth 0.0001 pence). Each cracker contains a paper hat (which you are supposed to wear) and a silly question and answer or joke (at which you are supposed to laugh).

Party-time

If invited to a Christmas party, wear your best clothes. Women can either look magnificent and formal, or cool and sexy. You can choose glossy material covered in so many sequins that you glitter like the Christmas tree, or a 'little black number' which shows as much as possible of your legs (wear black high heeled pumps). Men often wear waistcoats the same colour and pattern as gift wrapping paper. Little girls are dressed in creations with many frills.

Every year, almost everyone in Britain swears that they will not get caught up in the Christmas rush again, but inevitably they are. There are so many meals to cook, presents to buy, cards to write and relatives to visit that December is a stressful month.

Give a small present to your flatmates, and if you are invited to a Christmas party, take a present for the host and hostess as well as for their children. Children are often led to believe that 'Father Christmas' comes on a sledge with reindeer, and climbs down the chimney to deliver presents.

If you don't know someone well, here are some ideas for presents. They are not terribly exciting, but they are 'correct' and 'polite'. The recipients may wrap them up again and give them to someone else next year, or donate them to a raffle – but that's not your problem.

For women
- fragrant soap
- small gift basket with cosmetics
- flower vase
- box of chocolates
- pack of pretty handkerchiefs
- scarf
- ethnic costume jewellery

For women or men
- illustrated book
- pen in a gift box
- CD or music cassette

For children
- illustrated book (for the appropriate age group)
- pack of colour pencils.

If the flower vase, scarf or brooch was made in your home country, or if the book shows your home country, or the music is typical of your region, so much the better. It makes your gift more personal.

Consider taking a few gift items with you to Britain. This may be a problem if your luggage allowance is limited. But small items of costume jewellery, folk music tapes or scarves won't take up much space or weight.

Christmas Day and the following day (called Boxing Day) are public holidays – hardly anyone has to work (with some exceptions, such as hospital or hotel staff).

SENDING VALENTINE CARDS

There are many theories about who St Valentine really was, but there is little doubt that some of the customs go back to pagan times. You have to give your boyfriend/girlfriend/husband/wife a Valentine card on 14 February. You can give a small present, such as chocolates or flowers, too. However, flowers, especially red roses, cost several times more than normal just before St Valentine's Day, so you may be better off giving your beloved flowers at other times of the year!

There is also the delightful custom of sending anonymous cards. You can buy pre-printed cards (usually with kitschy pink teddy bears) or make your own. Disguise your handwriting or cut out words from newspapers to make up your message. Give the cards to a friend to post from a place with an unfamiliar post mark.

Send your cards to someone you love secretly, or just to a nice young man/woman who deserves a bit of flattery and joy. Young women (and indeed, most women and men) are flattered by anonymous Valentines.

COPING WITH APRIL FOOLS DAY

April Fools Day is the first day of April. Before noon, you can tell outrageous lies and play lots of tricks on friends, neighbours and colleagues. But beware: they'll try to make you the April Fool. After midday, it is generally accepted that anyone who tells a lie or plays a trick is an April Fool themselves.

Nobody knows if the word 'fools' should have an apostrophe, and if so, where. Newspapers and dictionaries can't agree on a standard spelling.

HALLOWE'EN AND GUY FAWKES

These two occasions get more and more confused. Hallowe'en is a pagan custom, and Guy Fawkes commemorates the historic 'gunpowder plot' of 5 November 1605, but many British people like to hold a party at the end of October or in early November and celebrate both occasions at once. There will be fireworks, large bonfires, fancy dress parties, and children knocking at your door dressed up as little horrors demanding 'trick or treat' *ie* unless you give them some coins or sweets they play a nasty trick on you. Have a few sweets ready on 31 October.

12

Getting Education and Training

CHOOSING THE RIGHT SCHOOL

In Britain you can choose between state schools and private schools (also confusingly called public schools). **Private schools** are supposed to offer better tuition because they have smaller class sizes and because they attract the best teachers, but you have to pay a high fee. Some of the private schools are boarding schools, which means that students live in the school.

State schools are free and chronically underfunded: teaching materials are often outdated, and there are not enough materials available. However, your children can get a good free education at a state school.

A new development is that of a **grant maintained** school. These schools get money from the state, but are responsible for their own budgeting.

Schools publish annual 'league tables', showing how well their pupils have done in exams, how much absenteeism there was, and so on. Every year the league tables make the newspaper headlines. The schools who did best use them to prove that they are the best schools. The schools who come at the bottom end of the league table protest that the wrong sort of achievements were tested and that the tables reflect neither true learning, nor the right skills.

Most schools in Britain are co-educational, that is, boys and girls are taught together. However, there are a few schools (especially private schools) which accept only boys or only girls.

School uniforms

Many British schools require that pupils wear a **school uniform**. For most state schools, this simply means, for example, navy blue jacket, navy blue skirt or trousers, navy blue sweater, plus white shirt and perhaps a tie.

Other schools' colours may be black, dark brown, dark green or grey. If the uniform is of such a plain standard colour, you can usually buy it from high street shops or by mail order. It gets more complicated when the uniform is of a specific cut and colour combination and you can obtain it from only one (expensive!) supplier.

You can buy school uniforms second hand from parents whose children have outgrown their uniform or left the school. There may be a school shop dealing in second hand uniforms and other equipment.

The school year
The academic year normally begins in September and is divided into three terms (autumn, spring and summer). Between the terms (in summer, at Christmas and at Easter) students are given several weeks' holiday. There are also some days off in the middle of each term.

Young children
If you have a toddler, you can join a parent and toddler group to give your child (and yourself) the chance to make friends. Parent and toddler groups usually meet once a week. Playgroups and kindergartens for pre-school children (usually age 3–5) may offer daily sessions. You will probably have to pay for such 'pre-school' facilities as very few free places are available.

At the age of five your child will start primary school. There is probably a primary school near where you live.

Secondary school
Secondary school education usually begins at age 11. To go to secondary school, a pupil may have to travel some distance. There are school buses (the pupil may be entitled to free transport), or parents from the same neighbourhood take turns to collect their children. This is called the 'school run'.

There is a confusing variety of secondary schools, such as comprehensive schools and grammar schools. Some are considered 'good schools', others are not. Ask around which schools in the area are 'good' – or consult the league tables.

Examinations
Students are about 16 when they take the GCSE (general certificate of secondary education) exams in several subjects. At least five GCSEs are needed to move on to higher education.

At the age of 18, students can take A level examinations in one or several subjects. Scotland has a separate education system which

uses slightly different terminology.
There are many more examinations and tests throughout school.

Foreign and international schools
There are some schools specially for foreign nationals, which can be useful if your children don't speak English well, or if you plan to return to your home country after a year or so. These schools are usually in London. Ask your embassy or high commission.

You can also study for an International Baccalaureate in East Sussex. This is an arrangement between the Pestalozzi International Village in Sedlescombe and Hastings College of Arts & Technology.

Checklist for choosing a school
1. Is there a school fee to pay? How much?

2. Is there a uniform? How much will this cost?

3. What extracurricular activities does the school offer? Will my children be able to pursue their hobbies?

4. How was the school doing in the last league tables?

5. How near is the school to our home?

6. Is there a school bus? If yes, does it stop near our home? If no, how are my children going to get to school and back?

GOING TO COLLEGE OR UNIVERSITY

Applying for a place
Universities in Britain usually comprise several smaller colleges, each specialising in a specific study area. Most universities are government-owned and you apply through a central application system. You have to apply in the autumn term to start in the following autumn.

Admission depends on your A-level results (or your country's equivalent, such as the Abitur) and possibly on an interview. If your A-levels are not as good as you expected, you may have to make new arrangements.

British universities require evidence that your English is good enough to follow the lessons. If your English skills are not up to that standard, you will have to complete a Foundation Year before you can enter your first university year of study. Some universities offer Foundation Year programmes – usually nine months long. It is not normally necessary to take the Foundation Year at the same university where you plan to study. Fees vary a lot. EF offers a Foundation Year course beginning in September and January, which takes place in London and is accepted by many UK universities.

You can find out more about studying in Britain with two other books from this series, *Going for Higher Education* and *Getting a Place at University.*

Qualifications
At college you can take A levels and diplomas. At university, the main qualifications are BA (Bachelor of Arts) or Bsc (Bachelor of Science), and MA (Master of Arts) or Msc (Master of Science).

Getting a scholarship
The British government and other organisations give some scholarships for international students. For example:

EU schemes
The European Union sponsors some students and academic staff from EU countries as well as from developing countries. Write to: The European Commission, Directorate General III, Rue de la Loi 200, B-1049 Brussels, Belgium.

Commonwealth Scholarship
For students from Commonwealth countries to research for postgraduate degrees at universities. About 400 scholarships each year. Apply through the Commonwealth Scholarship agency in your home country or write to: The Commonwealth Scholarship Commission, Association of Commonwealth Universities, 36 Gordon Square, London WC1H OPF.

British Council Fellowship Programme
For students who are likely to be influential in their professions and to promote an understanding of the UK. About 500 places each year, mostly for postgraduate studies and PhD research. Contact: Development and Training Services, British Council Fellowship Section, The British Council, Medlock Street, Manchester M15 4AA.

FCO British Chevening Scholarships
About 3,000 awards annually to people who are likely to become decision makers and opinion formers in countries with which the UK's economic relations are expected to develop. Mostly for postgraduate studies. Apply through the British Diplomatic Mission in your home country.

Technical Co-operation Training
About 4,000 awards annually for training in economic, social and technical fields, normally at postgraduate level. Write to: Education Department, Overseas Development Administration, 94 Victoria Street, London SW1E 5JL.

ODA Shared Scholarship Scheme
Two hundred awards each year for Commonwealth people for undergraduate or postgraduate studies in subjects relating to the economic and social development of the student's home country. Contact the British high commission or British Council in your home country.

The Sino-British Friendship Scholarship
Only for students from the PR China. Information from the British Council.

Fulbright Graduate Student Awards
Only for US graduate students for pre-doctoral study in the UK. Contact the Council for the International Exchange of Scholars, 3007 Tilden Street NW, Suite 5M, Washington DC20008-3009, USA.

For further information on these and other scholarships, read the leaflet *Scholarships for International Students*, published by UKCO-SA. The ministry of education in your home country can advise on UNESCO and WHO sponsored schemes.

Subscribing to UKCOSA

UKCOSA (The UK Council for Overseas Student Affairs) provides up-to-date information and advice to international students and to teachers who are working with foreign students. You can become a member and will receive regular newsletters and journals and discounts on UKCOSA publications.

Particularly useful are the guidance leaflets for students on subjects such as *Postgraduate study, Financial help, Scholarships for inter-national students, Choosing the right course.* A set of any three of these guidance notes costs £3 for non-members and £0.40 for members (see Useful Addresses).

For information on UKCOSA membership and a publications list, write to UKCOSA, 9–17 St Albans Place, London N1 0NX. Tel: (0171) 226 3762, Fax: (0171) 226 3373.

Further information
To find out more about going to school, college or university in Britain, read the book *How To Study & Live in Britain, A Handbook for Students from Overseas* by Jane Woolfenden.

STUDYING BY CORRESPONDENCE

It is possible to gain a university qualification by studying by correspondence with the Open University.

There are also private correspondence colleges which offer tuition in subjects as varied as Writing a Novel and Watercolour Painting. However, these don't offer qualifications.

One of the advantages of studying by correspondence (also called 'distance learning') is that you can begin your course while you are still in your home country.

Some useful addresses
Open University, PO Box 48, Milton Keynes MK7 6HN.
The Open Business School, 1 Cofferidge Close, Stony Stratford, Milton Keynes MK11 7BY.
The London School of Journalism, 1–4 Daniel Mews, Bathwick, Bath.
The Guild of Romance Writers Correspondence Course, Freepost PE 375, PO Box 95, Huntingdon, Cambridgeshire PE17 5EL.

TRAINING FOR A VOCATION

If you are interested in training with a company, get the booklet *Just the Job*, which is available free of charge from Jobcentres.

Many training schemes lead to NVQs (National Vocational Qualifications). For many fields of work NVQs are available at several levels. You can either start at NVQ level 1, then move on to NVQ level 2 and so on, or you can go straight into training for a higher level, if you have the necessary educational background.

Another group of qualifications is C&G (City and Guilds).

It is possible to take a course in the UK to train for a specific kind of work. Some courses lead to a diploma from the school, others to an accredited qualification. Many of these courses are geared especially towards international students, but you will need intermediate or advanced level knowledge of the English language. You have to budget for accommodation, meals, and living expenses as well as your course fees which can be expensive.

Here are some possibilities:

- Evendine Colleges in London offer certificate course at various levels in book-keeping, accounting, business administration, computing and information technology, secretarial skills, air fares and ticketing, as well as a flight attendants' diploma course.

- Cordon Bleu offers diploma courses in professional cooking, patisseries, and restaurant management. These courses take place in London.

- The Oxford Business College offers a marketing certificate course which has a practically oriented syllabus, as well as a nine-month academic course administered by the Institute of Commercial Management. This course is intended as an alternative to A-levels for entry into UK Higher Education, and students can enter it in September, January, April or July.

- Regent Language Training runs teacher training courses, for native speakers of English as well as non-native speakers. You will need previous teaching experience or qualifications to get on their specialist courses, which include teaching one-to-one and teaching business English.

- Eastbourne School of English also has teacher training courses, aimed at native and non-native speakers, at those new to the profession and those who are already teaching.

OPTING FOR ADULT EDUCATION

Here is a selection from the adult education programme of a small town, Rye (East Sussex), which will give you an idea of the variety: creative writing, writing for publication, improve your maths, English for speakers of other languages, silk painting, painting and drawing, watercolour painting, life drawing, French, German,

Italian, Spanish, car maintenance for women, astrology, aromatherapy, bridge, batik, computing, wordprocessing, Oriental dancing, traditional Chinese medicine, flower arranging, gardening, meditation, geography, papier mâché, patchwork and quilting, pottery, reflexology, curtain making, upholstery, yoga, teaching skills, biology, business studies, history, psychology, religious studies, law, book keeping, etching, literature, electrical installation, supervisory management, engineering and shorthand.

Many of these courses are available at beginner, intermediate and advanced level. Larger towns and cities have even wider programmes, ranging from video editing to plumbing, from music theory to hairdressing, from darkroom photo development to furniture restoration.

Here are some price examples, taken from the brochure of Ashford Adult Education Centre:

- Computing – Design your own World Wide Web Page, 5 weeks (2 hours per week) £41.
- Interior design, 11 weeks (2 hours per week) £24.50.
- Keep fit – Low impact aerobics, 12 weeks (1 hour per week) £29.
- Belly dancing – Turkish Gypsy (Rom) style, 1 day (4 hours) £15.

You may be entitled to a price reduction if you are unemployed.

The WEA (Workers Educational Association) and the University of the Third Age (U3A) offer courses and workshops for adults. Your local library will probably have their brochures.

CASE STUDIES

Hanna goes to London

'I came five years ago from the Netherlands to study music and singing on a two-year postgraduate course. I think the schools in Britain are more specialised, and I wanted to go to London to get a good education. I wanted to be where things happen, where there is a lot of competition, where the best music is. In London you can experience the best players reciting Shakespeare, and hear Placido Domingo singing. For a performing artist, London is at the same time a difficult and a stimulating place.

'I had a grant from the EC which part financed my studies. After finishing my studies, I set up a small cabaret ensemble with people who had been on the same course.'

Lynne studies in Scotland

'The college I was attending in the USA was part of the Great Lakes College Association which has a sister-school programme with Aberdeen, which kept the paperwork to a minimum. I knew I wanted to study in Britain, but sheer laziness decided where exactly I went. I would have been just as happy to go to England or Wales as to Scotland.'

Sigal tricks the security guard

'I was quickly offered a place at a few universities. I chose the City University. I spent the summer holidays working as a camp counsellor in the USA and received the paperwork there. Somehow I just didn't get a good vibe from the City on the whole, so when I returned to London, I called the University of Westminster. I had never been there, but I explained my situation. It was a week before the semester of the first year was scheduled to begin. I was so persistent, the university representative agreed to see me straight away. But in all the excitement I forgot her name and couldn't get into the building. I arrived at the psychology campus and the security guard wouldn't let me in. So I told him my story and asked him to list a few lecturers' names. I just said 'yes, this was the one I spoke to!' – although it wasn't. He called that extension and luckily it was engaged. I persuaded him to let me in. I knocked on all the doors of the psychology department and finally got through to a lecturer. I honestly had an interview on the spot and got a place. It was unbelievable. This lecturer is still my favourite person at the uni.'

POINTS TO CONSIDER

1. Will your children be able to follow the lessons in English language?

2. Would your children benefit from a private education? If yes, could you afford it?

3. Which adult education courses are available in your town? Which of them would be useful or interesting for you?

13

Travelling and Commuting

TRAVELLING BY AIR

Most international flights coming to Britain arrive either at London Heathrow or at London Gatwick. From Heathrow you can take the underground train or a special airport bus into London. The underground is quicker, but the bus offers a view of London. From Gatwick there is a special train called the Gatwick Express.

TAKING THE TRAIN

There is an adequate network of **railway lines** in Britain. Many trains are outdated and dirty, and in some areas they seem to be late all the time.

Station staff always announce the reason for the delay, for example, 'This is due to signalling problems', or 'This is because of engine problems'. Reasons for delays have also included 'leaves on the line' and 'the wrong type of snow'. You will hear British people making sarcastic comments if the train is late yet again.

British Rail is currently being privatised, that is split up and sold off to several private companies. It is hoped that this will make the train services more reliable, but many people fear that it will make rail travel more expensive than it is.

Never pay the normal ticket price if you can avoid it. There are so many special offers, discounts and reductions that nobody seems to pay full price. Before you buy a ticket, enquire what would be the cheapest way of getting to your destination and back. Travelling on weekends can be cheaper than on weekdays, and travelling after 9 or 10am can reduce the fare by 50 per cent. At very busy times, it is advisable to book your seat in advance.

Almost all railway lines lead to London. However, there is no one central London railway station. Several stations share that job: Paddington, Marylebone, Euston, St Pancras, Cannon Street, Charing Cross, Kings Cross, Waterloo and Victoria. If you want to travel from Hastings to Birmingham, you have to take a train to

London Charing Cross, then the underground to London Euston, and another train from there.

Some trains have doors which can be opened only from the outside. To get out, you have to open the window, reach out, then open the door.

GOING BY BUS

Buses are the public transport for short distances. In London, public transport buses are bright red; in other parts of the country they have other colours. You pay the driver when you get on the bus. Try to have the correct change. Drivers don't always have change, especially early in the morning.

In rural areas, public transport services are appalling. There are so few buses that it's impossible to rely on them to get anywhere. Therefore more and more people buy cars and avoid buses – and in consequence, the bus services are being cut back even further.

BY COACH

A coach is a bus, but for longer distances. The biggest network of coaches is the National Express. This is a cheap way of travelling long distances, in most cases costing far less than travelling by train. The coaches stop only in important towns. Most depart from London Victoria (the coach station, not the railway station). You buy the ticket from the ticket office. If you leave London in the morning, you are in Cornwall in the early evening.

USING THE UNDERGROUND

In London the quickest way of getting about is using the underground. Avoid travelling between 8 and 9am and between 5 and 6pm, when the carriages are crowded.

The lines are colour coded, and the colours are the same on every map you find. For example, the Central line is bright red, the Circle line is yellow, the Northern line is black. You can get a small underground map free from the ticket office. There are also large maps displayed near the ticket office and along the platforms.

You buy your ticket either from the ticket office or from a ticket machine. Some machines require you to have the correct change, others return change. You can also buy one-day or one-week travel cards which allow you to use the underground within a certain area as much as you wish. Ask at the ticket office.

Most underground stations have escalators. The rule is that you stand on the right side of the escalator. If you are in a hurry, you can walk on the left side.

DRIVING YOUR CAR

If you want to learn how to drive, you can practise with a friend who is an experienced driver and is over 21, as long as you display an L sign on the car. But it may be better to pay a driving instructor to make sure you are not learning bad habits.

You may be able to exchange your driving licence for a British driving licence (see page 92).

If you are used to driving on the right side of the road, driving on the left can be a problem. Some people adjust to the change easily, others take a long time. Take care especially after crossings, or when leaving petrol stations. This is when most people forget which side of the road they are meant to use. It is worth taking some extra driving lessons with an instructor, even if you don't need a whole course. For some, just two 'refresher lessons' are enough. Others (like me) need at least ten before they can drive confidently on the other side of the road. A driving lesson costs about £15. You can find addresses of instructors in the *Yellow Pages* under 'Driving Schools'.

Avoid taking your car into London. Finding your way through London is something which requires local knowledge as well as remarkable driving skills. You probably won't find a parking space anyway.

GOING BY BICYCLE

Unfortunately, Britain is not a bicycle-friendly country. There are very few cycling lanes. In London, you will see cyclists wearing masks because of the polluted air.

GOING ON FOOT

You are not allowed to walk across fields or through woods except where there is a 'Right of Way', a traditional path marked on maps. Rights of Way are usually signposted 'Public Footpath'. Follow the direction of the signs precisely. You may have to climb across stiles.

If you have to open gates, make sure you close them behind you.

CASE STUDIES

Claudia travels by train

'I remarked to fellow commuters waiting on the platform on how polite railway staff were, informing us about the reasons for the delay and apologising. This would not happen in Italy. But they didn't think this was a compliment. They started getting very sarcastic, saying that once I'd been in the country for a few weeks, I would be fed up with hearing apologies for delays. They were right.'

Lynne likes the public transport

'There's a decent system of public transportation here in Aberdeen, so even getting home after an evening in the pub isn't a problem. Although the reliability of public transport has taken a nose-dive in Scotland in the past few years, I still find it surprisingly reliable. It's perfectly possible to live without a car in most places.

'Watch out for traffic, cars parked in odd places, and absolutely insane passing practice! Lanes in roads are narrower than they are in the US, and the roads seldom have shoulders except the multi-lane motorways. The British treat a two-lane road as a three-lane, or even a four-lane, by parking on the sides and expecting two-way traffic to manouever around. This is a recipe for chaos. The national speed limit is 60mph on country roads and this is in no way a safe speed to go. Most of those roads would have a posted limit of 30mph in the US. But some of the locals happily travel at 60mph which can lead to bad crashes.

'Cars are expensive here. Once you've seen the price of gasoline – or rather 'petrol' – you will know just how incredibly spoilt Americans are. In America, we whine about having to pay more than a dollar a gallon, hah! It's about $5.20, here.'

Sigal won't take the train

'The transport is terrible. The trains can be very unreliable.'

POINTS TO CONSIDER

1. Will you need your own car in Britain?

2. Which types of public transport are you likely to use for commuting? How much will it cost?

14

Communicating

TALKING ABOUT THE WEATHER

Outside the UK, people seem to think that it rains constantly in this country. This is probably because the British talk so much about how awful the weather is. They are always complaining that it is too hot, too cold, too dry, too wet or too windy. It is never right.

If your English textbook at school contained the phrase 'Nice weather, isn't it?' (and most school textbooks do), it was probably written by a non-British national.

The most favourable comment you'll hear about the weather is: 'The weather is not too bad today, is it?' to which the accepted reply is: 'No, not too bad, although it could be better. This rain/snow/ wind/heat/drought isn't good for the roses/the apples/the dog/my nerves/my husband's arthritis.'

AVOIDING BRITISH TABOOS

There are a few subjects about which you, as a foreigner, should not talk. It is not forbidden, but the British may get very aggressive if you touch upon the subject and your opinion happens to differ from theirs. Just listen, and if asked, say 'I don't have an opinion myself, as I haven't been in the country for long, but I find what you are saying very interesting'.

Foxhunting
The people who are against foxhunting say it is cruel to the animals. Those in favour say that whole landscapes are preserved in their present form only because the owners use it for foxhunting. The conflict about foxhunting is sharper than about any other animal rights issue, possibly because the people who hunt foxes are perceived to be upper class and rich.

Dog mess
Should or should not dogs be permitted to lift their legs at every lamp post? Is it OK for owners to take their dogs to a children's playground, for them to use the sand pit there? Views differ, depending on whether someone has dogs or children. It may seem a harmless issue, but debates have escalated into violence. Stay clear.

Politics
The British complain about their government all the time. But they don't like foreigners doing the same! British people rarely discuss politics except with people who are known to hold the same views. If they find out that someone votes for another party, they can get hostile. If British people like you, they will automatically assume that you vote the same way they vote. Don't disillusion them. Keep quiet, even when asked which party you support and what your view is of the latest annual budget.

The underground
Don't talk to people on London underground trains. It is not done, even if you meet the same commuters day after day. The rules are a bit more relaxed on railway trains, but even there you should be careful. If they answer your questions in monosyllables, it means 'Leave me alone!'

BREAKING OUT OF ISOLATION

The greatest problem for many expatriates in Britain is the unwritten rule:

Don't talk to people until you have been introduced to them.

This can make life very difficult indeed. If you don't know anyone, there's nobody who can introduce you to other people. Some foreigners go nearly mad in this situation.

There are a few exceptions:

- If you own a **dog**, you can take it to the park and talk to other dog owners in the park. Consider yourself introduced by your dogs.

- If you have **toddlers** who play with other toddlers you can introduce yourself to the other parents. Consider yourself introduced by your toddlers.

- You can join a fitness or **sports club** and talk to anyone you meet there.

- You can ask people for instructions how to get to your destination. They will be helpful. But you have not been introduced, and they may ignore you the next time you see them.

What else can you do?
- Spread word that you are trying to meet people. If you appeal to your colleagues and flatmates to introduce you to others, they will probably help. These new acquaintances will not necessarily be the sort of people with whom you would normally make friends, but it's a start.

- Join groups and societies. As soon as you are a member, you can talk to other members.

- Join an adult education hobby course. But be patient, for the first few weeks people won't talk to each other.

- Go to the pub. You can talk to anyone else standing at the bar. However, they will probably say something like 'We must keep in touch and meet again' and deliberately forget to exchange phone numbers.

- Join an Anglo-International society (see page 164).

HAVING A TYPICAL CONVERSATION

After a few months or years in Britain, you know which questions to expect when you meet someone new. You'll know the answers by heart, and it can be difficult to keep up an enthusiastic smile, an interested tone of voice, when your brain is tempted to switch to autopilot!

Here are the typical questions you'll be asked, in the typical order:

1. Where do you come from?
2. Are you a student/an au pair?

3. What made you come here?
4. Why didn't you stay in America/Germany/Italy? How could you leave such a modern/rich/nice country?
5. How long have you been here?
6. Do you like it here?
7. How long are you here for?
8. Your English is very good. Where did you learn it?
9. Are you married to an Englishman/Englishwoman? The answer 'no' leads inevitably to the question of repetition (with a different intonation): What **made** you come here?
10. Where exactly in America/Germany/Italy do you come from?
11. I've got a cousin whose boyfriend's sister went to Germany 20 years ago. To Hintertupfelshausen. Do you know that place?
12. How do you like England/Britain? Be honest.

I have tried to break the routine by interrupting it with my own questions, or by giving unexpected answers. I tried (German) humour. I answered question number 1 with 'from Cranbrook' (my home), which made some people smile, but made others aggressive.

The reply to question number 8, 'Your English isn't bad either, where did you learn it?' doesn't appeal to the British sense of humour at all.

For number 3, it's better not to say: 'I wanted to go abroad, and the UK seemed the easiest option'. The British like to think that their country is the most appealing on earth, so say something flattering.

Question number 12 is a trap: the last thing they want is honesty at this early stage of acquaintance. You may get away with something non-committal such as 'interesting country'. But the best reply is 'I love the country, the language and the people. Only the weather could be better.' Sometimes it even makes them smile.

MAKING A PHONE CALL

Some phone boxes use **coins** (10p is the smallest coin they take), for others you need **phone cards**. You can buy phone cards at newsagents. If you phone someone, they won't always reply with their name (except if it's a business name). They will often just say 'Yes?' or 'Hello'.

You have to introduce yourself, and let them decide if they wish to talk to you.

 # Important telephone numbers

999 Emergency services. For example, in case of an accident or fire. No charge.

150 Customer service. For example, if you want to buy a telephone or have a line installed. No charge.

151 Fault reporting. For example, if a public telephone doesn't work. No charge.

100 UK operator

155 International operator

192 UK directory enquiries. To find out a UK number.

153 International directory enquiries. To find a telephone number abroad. No charge.

Other important phone numbers vary from area to area. You will find them listed in the front of your local telephone directory.

Fig. 8. Important telephone numbers.

To make a phone call abroad, dial 00, followed by the country code, followed by the area code and the number.

Figure 8 gives some useful telephone numbers.

GOING TO THE POST OFFICE

At the post office you can buy postage stamps and send letters and parcels. You can also send and receive telefaxes, buy some stationery, and pick up forms and advice brochures on anything from driving licence applications to income support.

For mail within the UK, there are two classes: first class and second. First class is usually delivered within a day or two, second class can take a few days. In December it can take longer, because of the Christmas post. A first class stamp for a letter of up to 60g costs 27 pence at the time of writing, and second class 19 pence. The stamps have their values printed on them, '27p' or '1st', '19p' or '2nd'.

For heavier letters, for mail abroad, for recorded mail and so on pick up the relevant leaflets from the post office.

CHECKLIST

1. Have I made a list of important phone numbers, such as emergency services, doctor and so on?

2. Have I obtained leaflets with up-to-date postal rates from the post office?

CASE STUDIES

Monica asks for directions

'My very first impression of Britain was very good: the people were so helpful. When I asked directions, they explained the way with all the details, then asked: "Do you understand? Yes? Would you like to repeat it so that I'm sure you've understood?" They took full responsibility for me finding my way.'

Antonio uses the church

'I found it difficult to make friends. I suppose I was too proud to admit that I was lonely. But finally I mentioned to a member of my church how difficult it was to make friends. He immediately introduced me to a lot of people.'

Deborah makes conversation
'One of my first impressions of Britain was that everyone I met said "But why did you leave such a modern, high tech, wonderful country like the USA to live here?"'

Lynne tries to rush friendships
'Making friends was difficult at first because I didn't have the cultural nuances down and was too direct. I also tried to rush into friendships a lot more quickly than people in Scotland are used to doing. However, now I just wait to get to know people better, and it makes starting a friendship a lot easier. When I come back to visit America now, people find me more reserved than I used to be.

'I'd advise Americans to tone it down. Britons find Americans incredibly loud, brash and arrogant. Lower your tone of voice, that will help people deal with you. Don't try to strike up conversations with strangers who just happen to be standing in line with you. They don't know you and you will just make them nervous. Don't volunteer yourself into other people's situations even if you think you can help, except in an emergency like a car accident. Don't assume that America is the greatest country in the world – you'll meet a lot of people who don't agree. Learn to laugh at yourself. Oh yes, and learn to pronounce Edinburgh as 'Edinboro' not 'Edinburg'.

'Whatever your nationality, be aware that the UK can be quite xenophobic at times. Just be prepared for the press accusing you of draining the system of resources, and the possibility of racism in everyday life.'

Fiona recommends travelling
'I had no problem making friends. Living on a Scottish country estate we were all a bit isolated, but that just meant you had to work harder. At the end we had a great crowd and we would meet up every weekend. I think the main thing when you come over here is to have an open mind, be relaxed and very carefree. You need to get as much travel in as possible and expect to meet some of the most amazing people.'

Zinga finds making friends difficult
'Everything about life is different to how I experienced it back home: food, relationships, attitudes...It's difficult to make friends because of the different attitudes to friendship here. In Tunisia, a friend is like a brother, or more. Here, people are more casual. I don't find

English people very friendly either.'

Carina appreciates the social niceness

'Some words – such as 'love' – have strong meanings in Swedish but are used very casually in English. I had to learn to take things not quite so seriously.

'I like the lack of conformity on many levels, the social niceness of day-to-day contact with people you don't know well, the casual chattiness that makes things flow a bit smoother.'

POINTS TO CONSIDER

1. Who do you know who could introduce you to other people? Make a list of colleagues, friends, flatmates, neighbours, fellow expatriates, members of your church and so on.

2. What else can you do to break the circle of isolation? Consider several possibilities.

15

Staying Healthy

COPING WITH YOUR FIRST MONTHS

You will be under enormous stress during your first months in the UK. It is inevitable that one or more of the following factors will put you under emotional or mental strain:

- you are homesick

- you are depressed because you can't find a job

- you lose your self-confidence because you don't succeed in your job-hunt and other matters

- you are worried because your money is running out

- you miss your family/your spouse/your lover

- you may encounter prejudice or racial discrimination

- you are having difficulty making friends because the British are so reserved

- you have nobody to talk to

- you doubt if you have made the right decision in coming to Britain.

But your boss, colleagues and new acquaintances expect you to be strong, cheerful, sparkling, productive, meeting the challenge.

Even if you are forced to act out this role, it is essential that you are honest to yourself. If you are lonely, depressed or worried, admit it. Talk to your mirror image or write your feelings down. If you bottle them up and deny them, they will suddenly burst out, and you may have a nervous breakdown or become very ill.

Remind yourself that these feelings are normal for someone in your situation. Find someone to talk to. A fellow expat, maybe from your own country, is often the best person.

If you find you are near breaking point, seek help (see page 41).

Take care of yourself. Do something you really enjoy, something you have always wanted to do. Pamper yourself as far as time and financial limits allow (see page 119).

This mental adjustment comes at a time when you have to adjust physically, too. The following may affect your physical and mental well-being:

- the different climate

- illnesses against which most British people have built up immunity but to which your body is susceptible

- food to which you are not used

- you don't have access to the medicines you are used to

- you don't know how to find/choose/pay for medical care.

Many people who go to live in a new country ignore the needs and warning signals of their bodies during the first few months, thinking 'I have more important matters to deal with'. This is dangerous. If you become physically ill, you won't be able to deal with those 'important matters' at all.

KEEPING WARM

If you come from a warmer country, the cold and wet climate in the UK can make you ill. Here are some tips how to keep warm and healthy.

Dressing warmly

- Dress warmly with **gloves**, **hat**, **cap** or **scarf**, even for a short trip. One third of the body heat gets lost through the head.

- **Several thin layers** of clothing keep you warmer than one thick layer. They have the advantage that you can take off some layers when you go indoors, or if it gets warmer in the afternoon. For example, you could wear: a sleeveless vest, a short-sleeved T-shirt, a long-sleeved T-shirt, a thin jersey, and a jacket.

- Many people forget to **keep their legs warm**. Buy long underpants ('longjohns') and wear a long jacket or a coat.

- Wear **thick-soled shoes** and thick socks.

- **Natural fibres** such as wool, cotton and silk keep you warmer than man-made fibres such as acrylics or nylon, and they allow your skin to breathe.

- Buy **thermals**, that's underwear, gloves and so on, made from hollow fibres which provide extra insulation.

Other tips for keeping warm

- Get some **exercise** every day.

- Keep **curtains closed** at night to keep warmth in.

- Opening all windows wide for five minutes to get fresh air is more energy-saving than keeping one window open a little all the time.

- Try to keep a **constant temperature** of about 21°C (70°F) in your rooms. Buy a room thermometer to check the temperature.

- Have **several meals**, including at least one hot meal, every day and drink a lot of water and soft drinks.

- Buy a small **electric heater** in case your central heating system breaks down.

- Dark skinned people suffer particularly from lack of sunshine. Make a point of **going for a walk** or sitting in a park whenever the sun is shining. Sunbeds can also compensate to some extent.

PREVENTING COLDS AND FLU

The flu (influenza) is an illness which comes in many variations. It can spread like an epidemic and leave the body weakened and vulnerable. Colds on the other hand are seldom dangerous, but they are still unpleasant. The symptoms, causes, prevention and treatment for flu and for a cold are similar.

You are likely to catch a cold or flu if you spend some time close to a person who is infected. However, you are more susceptible if your body's resistance is weak – for example, if your diet doesn't contain enough vitamins, if you don't dress warmly, if you are worried or stressed. If there is a flu or cold going round, listen to the warning signals of your body, and consider taking extra vitamins.

Spotting the symptoms

Symptoms include sneezing, runny nose, aching limbs, headache, sinusitis (pain in the forehead or to the left or right of your nose), sore throat, thirst, raised temperature, fever.

As soon as you notice the first symptoms, you should avoid stress and take a rest. Take a hot bath, go to bed early, drink a lot of water, herbal tea and fruit juice, and eat fruit and vegetables. If you are careful, you may feel better after just a couple of days.

If you get ill, take time off work. Stay at home. It would not be fair to pass on your illness to your colleagues at work, or to the other people on the bus or train. Once the flu or cold has taken hold, it will take at least five to seven days to pass. There is nothing you can do to shorten the period. You can only ease the symptoms, and prevent complications.

Try the following:

- Drink as much as possible (but only very little alcohol).

- Eat plenty of fruit.

- Rosehip, camomile, lime and peppermint tea are traditional herbal remedies.

- Evaporate a few drops of eucalyptus, lavender or tea tree oil in an essential oil 'burner'.

- Take aspirin or paracetamol tablets.

- Heat grapefruit or lemon juice (but don't boil it), add some honey, and drink it hot.

- The most popular cold remedy in Britain is paracetamol powder with lemon flavour, to be prepared as a hot drink. They are available under several different brand names, and you can buy them in corner shops, supermarkets, from chemists and pharmacies.

- Peel a small piece of ginger root, chop it, pour hot water over it, and let it stand for a few minutes before drinking it.

- Garlic, honey and onions are foods supposed to strengthen the body against colds and flu.

- If you are worried or have any questions, or if you need confirmation that you are ill for your employer, see your doctor at once.

TREATING HEADACHES AND MIGRAINES

Headaches can be triggered by many things, including stress and polluted air. If you have a headache for the first time, or if your headaches are more severe than you are used to in your home country, see a doctor.

The typical British remedy would be aspirin or paracetamol tablets. These are general painkillers, but are particularly useful for headaches. They are quite cheap and you can buy them not only in pharmacies and at chemists, but also in supermarkets and corner shops.

WOMEN'S HEALTH

For PMS (premenstrual syndrome) many British women take capsules of evening primrose oil.

Many women in Britain suffer from vaginal thrush. That's an infection you can catch when you use public toilets or swimming pools. The symptoms are a thick discharge and itching in and around the vagina which gets worse. Treat it at once; don't wait for it to get worse.

Because so many women catch it and cannot bear to wait several days for a doctor's appointment, remedies are now sold over the counter in pharmacies. If you find it embarrassing to explain the symptoms to a male pharmacist with a queue of people waiting behind you, just show the paragraph in this book, and the pharmacist will know what is required.

You can also ease the symptoms or cure the problem in the early stages by adding vinegar to cold washing water and by avoiding hot water and soap for a while. Use two drops of tea tree oil on a tampon. Eat plenty of natural live yoghurt and avoid sugar. Don't wear tight synthetic underwear.

KEEPING CLEAN

Everyone is expected to take a bath or a shower every day. British houses and flats are more likely to be equipped with baths than with showers.

You can buy tampons and sanitary towels in several sizes and shapes. Popular tampon brands are Lil-Lets and Tampax. You get them from pharmacies, chemists, supermarkets and corner shops.

Many public toilets have vending machines.

Women are expected to shave their legs and underarms. It's considered unhygienic if they don't. Strangely, nobody seems to find anything unhygienic about men's hairy legs and armpits.

Men and women should use a deodorant once or twice a day.

Perfumes are worn only by women, although men can use a fragrant aftershave. Young men can wear perfumes for special occasions in the evenings.

TAKING CONTRACEPTIVES

If you want to take the pill, you have to go to your doctor or to the family planning clinic to get a prescription. Your blood pressure, among other things, will be tested. You can get the pill free of charge, but you have to go for a repeat examination every six months or so.

Condoms can be bought everywhere. Many people prefer to buy them in supermarkets with their weekly shopping. Like cigarettes and sweets, condom packets are usually on display near the cash till. Just put them in your basket or trolley. Many British women buy condoms openly, so there is no need to be embarrassed. Condom vending machines are placed in many men's and some women's toilets.

Other contraceptives, such as the sponge or pessaries, can be bought in pharmacies. If you are uncertain which method is best for you, or if you consider getting an IUD (coil), discuss it with your doctor.

UNDERSTANDING THE NHS

The NHS is the National Health Service. It pays for some prescriptions and treatments, and gives a contribution to some others. It seems that every year the benefits from the NHS get fewer.

You are entitled to a **health check** when you register with a new doctor, to a **smear test** every three years (women), and to **free advice** when you are ill. You are also entitled to **essential operations**, but there can be a long waiting list. You may have to wait for several months or years.

You have to pay for prescribed medicines, dental services, eye tests and spectacles, although you can get these free or at a reduced rate if you are a child or on a very low income.

There is a lot of dissatisfaction among the British about the way

NHS services have been cut back.

SEEING A DOCTOR

As soon as you have settled in, you should register with an NHS doctor. Don't wait until you are ill. Note that some NHS doctors also take private patients, so make sure you are treated as an NHS patient – otherwise you may have to pay a lot for the treatment. Most NHS doctors have a schedule which allows them to spend just seven to ten minutes on each patient. This is hardly enough for you to explain what's wrong with you, let alone for the doctor to examine you thoroughly and to give detailed advice. The atmosphere can be impersonal and rushed.

It helps if you don't store up several problems for each visit, and if you think in advance what you are going to say. Explain your symptoms clearly and briefly, or write them down for your doctor to read.

Smear tests, vaccinations and general health checks are performed by a practice nurse.

Opticians
For eye-tests and spectacles, you go to an optician. You will have to pay for the prescription and the glasses.

Dentists
It can be difficult to find an NHS dentist. All dentists think they are underpaid and therefore prefer practising privately. Some towns have no NHS dentist at all, so that you are forced to seek private treatment.

Some dentists take NHS as well as private patients. Private patients get better treatment, but it is more expensive. Even NHS treatment and check-ups cost money. When you register with a dentist, they will give a first check-up, and charge you for it.

Pharmacies and chemists
Although you can buy some general medicines in supermarkets and corner shops you have to go to a chemist or to a pharmacy for most remedies. They have a wide range of medicines available for everything from digestive trouble to hayfever. The pharmacy is also the place where you hand in your doctor's prescription to buy your medicine.

Alternative medicine
Especially in towns you will also find practitioners of alternative medicine, such as homeopaths, herbalists, kineseologists, reflexologists, aromatherapists, hypnotherapists and so on. Check your local *Yellow Pages* under 'Therapists'.

If you want to use alternative medicine for self-treatment, you can buy remedies either in a pharmacy or in a health food shop.

Further reading
The following booklets and leaflets may be useful:

Winter Warmth, free of charge from Keep Warm Keep Well, FREEPOST, London SE5 7BP. This booklet is available in English, Welsh, Chinese, Greek, Polish, Turkish, Bengali, Gujarati, Hindi, Punjabi and Urdu.

Help with NHS costs, a brochure which advises on entitlement to free or reduced-rate prescriptions, spectacles, eye-tests, dental treatment and so on. Free from your post office.

Sick or disabled? A guide to benefits if you are sick or disabled for a few days or more. Free from your post office or Social Security office.

CHECKLIST

1. Have I registered with a doctor?

2. Have I registered with a dentist?

3. Do I know where the nearest pharmacy is?

4. Do I know which medicines are available at the nearest shop?

5. Do I know the opening hours of the doctor's and dentist's surgeries and the pharmacy?

6. Have I worked out how to get there by public transport?

7. Do I have the doctor's and dentist's phone number at hand?

CASE STUDIES

Hanna goes home for treatment

'I have lived in Britain for five years now, but I haven't found a dentist yet who is as good as the one I used in the Netherlands. I go to a British dentist for the six-monthly check-ups, but whenever I need treatment or repairs, I go to my Dutch dentist.'

Ursula gets fed up

'I'm fed up with British dentists. I've been to five dentists, and every one moaned about how little they earn compared with their German counterparts. They tell me that treatment won't be as good as in Germany because the NHS pays them only for so many minutes. I wish they'd spend these minutes treating my teeth instead of moaning!

'I've asked my current dentist repeatedly not to talk about the wonderful income of German dentists. But he brings up the subject every time. I'm fed up.'

Ozel never sees the same doctor

'I registered with a woman doctor at the local surgery. I prefer certain gynaecological examinations to be done by a woman, and in Turkey I had a woman doctor, too. The receptionist was understanding, and I was seen by a woman doctor.

'But although I've been with the surgery for several years now and have had treatment for various ailments, I never saw her again. Each time I was treated by a different doctor, and always a man. They just pass my medical file to whichever doctor is free.

'Recently I had to provide "the signature of the doctor who has known you for at least five years" to prove my identity. This is a joke. None of the doctors at the surgery would recognise me.'

Michael waits for the specialist

'Ever since coming to Britain, I've had a knee problem. I am in severe pain for several days, then it is alright for a few weeks, comes again for a few days, and so on. X-rays and repeated examinations didn't show the cause, so my doctor referred me to a specialist. I had to wait seven months for the appointment. When I finally saw him, he said "Where does it hurt just now?" "Just now, not at all," I replied truthfully. "Why are you here then? You are wasting my time and NHS money. Come again when the pain is there."'

'I said I had waited half a year for the appointment and it was impossible to predict in advance on which date the pain would occur. But he refused to examine my knee.'

Lynne tries to stay warm

'The weather in Scotland is just sodding miserable. Never under-estimate the pervasive chill and damp here. Also, it rains a lot, worse than in Seattle, and all year round. Eventually the chill just soaks right through you. I don't like having to wear a jacket, gloves and a scarf in midsummer.

'Americans complain if they have to keep their houses at 68°F (20°C) for energy reasons. Here, that temperature is considered fairly warm. Many people keep their houses at 65°F (19°C). I spend a lot of time wrapped in multiple layers of clothing and huddled by the radiators. Oh yes, and another thing: People here think they have the hang of centrally heated houses but I don't think so!'

Sigal suffers from British weather

'The weather in London, the lack of sun, gets me down a lot of the time, and I am often sick.'

POINTS TO CONSIDER

1. Does the NHS offer more, or less, than the state health service in your home country? How will the difference affect you?

2. Would it be worth taking out private health insurance, or private dental insurance?

3. Could it be a solution to put aside a lump sum, or a monthly amount, to pay for medicines, dentist's bills and hospital stays? If yes, how much do you think this should be for yourself and your family?

Glossary

BA:	Bachelor of Arts (university degree)
BSc:	Bachelor of Science (university degree)
BT:	British Telecom (telephone services)
D.o.B.:	Date of Birth
DTP:	Desktop publishing
EU:	European Union
GB:	Great Britain
GCSE:	General Certificate of Secondary Education
JCWI:	Joint Council for the Welfare of Immigrants
MA:	Master of Arts (university degree)
MSc:	Master of Science (university degree)
MD:	managing director
MP:	Member of Parliament
M.P.:	medical practitioner (doctor)
NHS:	National Health Service
NI:	National Insurance
NVQ:	National Vocational Qualification
PA:	personal assistant
p.a.:	per annum (wages per year)
PhD:	Doctor of Philosophy (academic title)
RSA:	Royal Society of Arts
sae:	stamped addressed envelope
s/h:	shorthand
temp:	temporary
UK:	United Kingdom of Great Britain and Northern Ireland
UKCOSA:	United Kingdom Council for Overseas Student Affairs
WI:	Women's Institute
WP:	wordprocessing
w.p.m.:	words per minute (typing/shorthand speed)
YHA:	Youth Hostels Association
YMCA/YWCA:	Young Men's/Women's Christian Association

Further Reading

Culture Shock! Britain, Terry Tan (Graphic Arts Center Publishing Company, 1992).

How To Study and Live in Britain, A Handbook for Students from Overseas, Jane Woolfenden (How To Books 1990).

Living and Working in Britain, David Hampshire (Survival Books 1991).

The Xenophobe's Guide to the English, Antony Miall (Ravette 1993).

Immigration and Nationality Law Handbook (JWCI 1995).

Getting a Place at University, Gerald Higginbottom, (How To Books).

Going for Higher Education, Gerald Higginbottom (How To Books).

Writing a CV that Works, Paul McGee (How To Books).

A series of useful leaflets for students are avaiable from UKCOSA, 9–17 St Albans Place, London N1 0NX. They cost £3 for any three leaflets of your choice, or £50 for a set of 21 leaflets. Here is a selection of titles: *Accommodation, Choosing the right course, Course fees and grants, Council tax, Keeping healthy, Students and employment, Students and immigration, Preparing to study, Postgraduate study, Address list for international students, Learning English in the UK, European mobility and exchange schemes, Arriving in the UK, EEA students, Financial help for students. Scholarships for international students.*

The following factsheets are available from the Joint Council for the Welfare of Immigrants, 115 Old Street, London EC1V. The JCWI also publishes booklets and books. For a complete list of materials available and prices, send a stamped addressed envelope.

How to sponsor your children to come to the UK, How to sponsor someone wanting to visit the UK, Useful addresses and telephone numbers, How to sponsor dependent parents and grandparents for settlement in the UK, How to sponsor your husband/wife to come to the UK.

Useful Addresses

EMBASSIES, HIGH COMMISSIONS AND CONSULATES IN BRITAIN

Embassy of the Republic of Afganistan, 31 Prince's Gate, London SW7 1QQ. Tel: (020) 7589 889.

Algerian Embassy, 54 Holland Park, London W11 3RS. Tel: (020) 7221 7800.

American Embassy, 24 Grosvenor Square, London W1 AE. Tel: (020) 7499 9000.

Embassy of the Argentine Republic, 53 Hans Place, London SW1X 01A. Tel: (020) 7584 6494.

Australian High Commission, Australia House, Strand, London WC28 4LA. Tel: (020) 7379 4334.

Austrian Embassy, 18 Belgrave Mews West, London SW1X 8HU. Tel: (020) 7235 3731. Fax: (020) 7235 8025.

Embassy of Belgium, 103 Eaton Square, London SW1W 9AB. Tel: (020) 7470 3700. Fax: (020) 7259 6213.

Brazilian Embassy, 32 Green Street, Mayfair, London W1Y 4AT. Tel: (020) 7499 0877.

Canadian High Commission, MacDonald House, 1 Grosvenor Square, London W1X OAB. Tel: (020) 7258 6600.

Embassy of the People's Republic of China, 49–51 Portland Place, London WIN 4JL. Tel: (020) 7636 9375.

Cyprus High Commission, 93 Park Lane, London W1Y 4ET. Tel: (020) 7499 8272.

Embassy of the Arab Republic of Egypt, 26 South Street, London W1Y 8EL. Tel: (020) 7499 2401.

German Embassy, 23 Belgrave Square, London SW1X 8PZ. Tel: (020) 7235 5033.

Embassy of Greece, 1a Holland Park, London W1 3TP. Tel: (020) 7727 3071. Fax: (020) 7727 8960.

Indian High Commission, India House, Aldwych, London WC2. Tel: (020) 7836 8484.

Embassy of Israel, 2 Palace Green, Kensington, London W84 QB. Tel: (020) 7957 9500.

Italian Embassy, 14 Three Kings Yard, London W1Y 2EH.

Embassy of Japan, 101 Piccadilly, London W1V 9FN. Tel: (020) 7465 6500.

Luxembourg Embassy, 27 Wilton Crescent, London SW1X 8SD. Tel: (020) 7235 6961.

Royal Netherlands Embassy, 38 Hyde Park Gate, London SW7 5DP. Tel: (020) 7584 5040. Fax: (020) 7581 3450.

New Zealand High Commission, New Zealand House, Haymarket, London SW1Y 4TQ. Tel: (020) 7930 8422.

Royal Norwegian Embassy, 25 Belgrave Square, London SW1X 8QD. Tel: (020) 7235 7151. Fax: (020) 7245 6993.

High Commission of Pakistan, 36 Lowndes Square, London SW1 9JN. Tel: (020) 7235 2044.

Embassy of the Russian Federation, 13–15 Kensington Palace Gardens, London W84 QX. Tel: (020) 7229 3628.

High Commission for the Republic of Singapore, 9 Wilton Crescent, London SW1X 8SA. Tel: (020) 7235 8315.

South African High Commission, South Africa House, Trafalgar Square, London WC2N 5DP. Tel: (020) 7930 4488.

Spanish Embassy, 24 Belgrave Square, London SW1X 8QA. Tel: (020) 7235 7537.

Spanish General Consulate, 20 Draycott Place, London SW1A. Tel: (020) 7594 0127.

Swiss Embassy, 16–18 Montagu Place, London W1H 2BQ. Tel: (020) 7723 0701.

Thai Embassy, Princes Gate, London 1PT. Tel: (020) 7584 2384.

INTERNATIONAL FRIENDSHIP AND CULTURAL EXCHANGE

Anglo-Austrian Society, 46 Queen Anne's Gate, London SW1H 9AU. Tel: (020) 7584 8653. Fax: (020) 7225 0470.

Anglo-Belgian Club, 60 Knightsbridge, London SW1X 7LF. Tel: (020) 7235 2121.

Anglo-Belgian Society, Linden 45, West Common, Haywards Heath, West Sussex RH16 2AJ. Tel: (0144) 4452183.

Anglo-Hellenic League, Flat 4, 68 Elm Park Gardens, London SW10 9PB.

The Anglo-Norse Society c/o the Norwegian Embassy (see under 'Embassies').

The Anglo-Netherlands Society, PO Box 68, Unilever House, London EC4P 4BQ.

Anglo-Spanish Society, 344 Westbourne Park Rd, London W11 1TQ. Tel: (020) 7823 7209.

The Anglo-Swiss Society, 2 The Mill Yard, Wickhambreaux, Canterbury, Kent CT3 1RQ. Tel: (01227) 721855.

British-Greek Cultural Friendship Association, United Standard House, 6 Middlesex Street, London E17 NEP.

The British-Luxembourg Society, c/o Mr George Kieffer, Tangle Trees, 120 Mountnessing Road, Billericay, Essex CM12 9HA. Tel: (01277) 650605.

Consul of Spanish Residents, 56 Erskine Crescent, Ferry Lane, London N17 9PA. Tel: (020) 8808 5654.

The Dutch Club, 60 Knightsbridge, London SW1.

The Finnish Institute in London, 35–36 Eagle Street, London WC1R 4AJ. Tel: (020) 7404 3309. Fax: (020) 7404 8893.

The Finnish Seamen's Mission, 33 Albion Street, London SE16 1JG.

Franco-British Society, 623 Linen Hall, 162–168 Regent Street, London W1R 5TB. Tel: (020) 7734 0815.

Greek Society of Professionals & Scientists in Great Britain, PO Box 1007, London W2 4PF.

The Hellenic Centre, 16–18 Paddington Street, London W1.

Institut Français D'Ecosse, 13 Randolph Crescent, Edinburgh EH3 7TT.

Institut Français D'Ecosse, 7 Bowmont Gardens, Glasgow G12 9LR.

Institut Français du Royaume-Uni, 17 Queensberry Place, London SW7 2DT.

Instituto Cervantes, 22–23 Manchester Square, London W1M 5AP. Tel: (020) 7935 1518.

Italian Cultural Institute, 39 Belgrave Square, London SW1. Tel: (020) 7235 1461.

Londres Accueil, 17 Queensberry Place, London SW7 2DT. Tel: (020) 7823 9947.

The Royal Belgian Benevolent Society in London, 60 Knightsbridge, London SW1X 7LF.

Norwegian Club, Norway House, 21/24 Cockspur Street, London SW1Y 5BN. Tel: (020) 7930 4084. Fax: (020) 7930 7786.

Vereniging Neerlandia c/o 5 The Knoll, Ealing, London W13.

GOVERNMENT DEPARTMENTS

Department for Environment, Food and Rural Affairs, Government Buildings, Hook Rise South, Tolworth, Surbiton, Surrey KT6 7NF. Tel: 0870 241 1710. e-mail: *pets@ahvg.maff.gsi.gov.uk www.maff.gov.uk/uk/animalh/quarantine*

Bwyrdd yr Iaith Cymraeg (Welsh Language Board), Market Chambers, 5–7 St Mary Street, Cardiff CF1 2AT.

Central Office of Information, Hercules Road, London SE1 7DU.

Central Statistical Office, Millbank Tower, Millbank, London SW1P 4QQ.

Charity Commissioners for England and Wales, St Alban's House, 57/60 Haymarket, London SW7 4QX.

Customs and Excise, 7th Floor East, New King's Beam House, 22 Upper Ground, London SE1 9PJ.

Cygnor Celfryddydau Cymru (Arts Council of Wales), 9 Museum Place, Cardiff CF10 3NX.

Data Protection Registrar's Office, Wycliffe House, Water Lane, Wilmslow SK9 5AF.

Ministry of Defence, Main Building, London SW1A 2BH.

Department of Economic Development (Northern Ireland), Netherleigh, Massey Avenue, Belfast BT4 2JP.

Department of Education (Northern Ireland), Rathgael House, Balloo Road, Bangor, County Down.

Department for Education and Skills, Education Section, Public Enquiry Unit, Sanctuary Buildings, Great Smith Street, London SW1P 3BT.

Department for Education and Employment, Employment Section, 236 Grays Inn Road, London WC1X 8HL.

General Teaching Council for Scotland, Clerwood House, 96 Clermiston Road, Edinburgh EH12 6UT.

Office of Electricity Regulation, Public Affairs, Hagley House, Hagley Road, Edgbaston, Birmingham B16 8QG.

Office of Electricity Regulation (Northern Ireland), Brookmount Buildings, 42 Fountain Street, Belfast BT1 5EE.

Employment Service, St Vincent House, Orange Street, London WC2H 7HY.

Department of the Environment, 2 Marsham Street, London SW1P 3PY.

Department of the Environment (Northern Ireland), Clarence Court, 10–18 Adelaide Street, Belfast BT2 8CB.

Export Credits Guarantee Department, 2 Exchange Tower, Harbour Exchange Square, London E14 9GS.

Office of Fair Trading, Field House, 15/25 Bream's Buildings, London EC4A 1PR.

Department of Finance and Personnel (Northern Ireland), Rosepark House, Upper Newtownards Road, Belfast BT4 3NR.

Foreign and Commonwealth Office, King Charles Street, London SW1A 2AH.

Department of Health, Richmond House, 79 Whitehall, London SW1A 2NS.

Health & Safety Executive, Sheffield Information Centre, Broad Lane, Sheffield S3 7HQ.

Health & Social Services Department (Northern Ireland), Castle Buildings, Stormont, Belfast BT4 3SG.

DHSS Agencies (Northern Ireland), Great Northern Tower, 17 Victoria Street, Belfast BT2 7AD.

Social Security Agency, Block A, Castle Buildings, Stormont Estate, Belfast BT4 3RA.

HMSO (Her Majesty's Stationery Office), St Crispins, Duke Street, Norwich NR3 1PD.

Home Office, Information & Library Services, Queen Anne's Gate, London SW1H 9AT.

Inland Revenue, South West Wing, Bush House, London WC2B 4RD.

HM Land Registry, 32 Lincoln's Inn Fields, London WC2A 3PH.

Lord Chancellor's Department, 6th Floor South, Trevelyan House, 30 Great Peter Street, London SW1P 2BY.

Court Service, Trevelyan House, Code Unit, 30 Great Peter Street, London SW1P 2BY.

Department of National Heritage, Library & Public Enquiry Unit, Lower Ground Floor, 2-4 Cockspur Street, London SW1Y 5DH.

National Lottery Office, 2 Monck Street, London SW1P 2BQ.

Northern Ireland Office, c/o PAGAB, Stormont, Belfast BT4 3SG.

Ordnance Survey (Maps), Romsey Road, Maybush, Southampton SO16 4GU.

Overseas Development Administration, Abercombie House, Eaglesham Road, East Kilbride G75 8EA.

HM Paymaster General's Office, Sutherland House, Russell Way, Crawley RH10 1UZ.

Public Records Office, Kew, Richmond, Surrey TW9 4DU.

Scottish Office, Victoria Quay, Edinburgh EH6 6QU.

Department of Social Security, DSS Headquarters, 1–11 John Adam Street, London WC2N 6HT.

DSS Benefits Agency, Quarry House, Leeds LS2 7UA.

DSS Contributions Agency, DSS Central Office, Newcastle, NE98 1YX.

Child Support Agency, DSS Central Office, Newcastle, NE98 1YX.

Department of Trade and Industry, Lower Ground Floor, 1 Victoria Street, London SW1H 0ET.

Department of Transport, Public Enquiry Unit, Greatminster House, 76 Marsham Street, London SW1P 4DR.

Scottish Arts Council, 12 Manor Place, Edinburgh EH3 7DD.

Scottish Qualifications Authority, Hanover House, 24 Douglas Street, Glasgow G2 7NQ.

Scottish Trade International, 120 Bothwell Street, Glasgow G2 7JP.

Treasury, Communications Division, HM Treasury, Parliament Street, London SW1P 3AG.

Office of Water Services, Centre City Tower, 7 Hill Street, Birmingham B5 4UA.

Welsh Office, Cathays Park, Cardiff CF1 3NQ.

Office of Population Censuses & Surveys, St Catherine's House, 10 Kingsway, London WC2B 6JP.

EDUCATION AND TRAINING

The British Accreditation Council for Independent Further and Higher Education, 27 Marylebone Road, London NW1 5JS.

British Council Education Information Service, 10 Spring Gardens, London SW1A 2BN.

Cordon Bleu, 114 Marylebone Lane, London W1U 2HH. Tel: (020) 7935 3503. Fax: (020) 7935 7621. *london@cordonbleu.net*

Eastbourne School of English, 8 Trinity Trees, Eastbourne, East Sussex BN21 3LD. Tel: (01323) 721759. Fax: (01323) 639271. *http://www.esdoe.co.uk* e-mail: *english@esoe.co.uk*

EF International Language Schools, 1–3 Farman Street, Hove, East Sussex BN3 1AL. Tel: (01273) 201 420. Fax: (01273) 448 566. *ils.uk.agents@ef.com*

Evendine College, 34/36 Oxford Street, London W1D 1AY. Tel: (020) 7636 5656. Fax: (020) 7636 5454. *evendine@evendine.com*

Evendine College, 227/229 Tottenham Court Road, London W1P 9AE. Tel: (020) 7580 1989. Fax: (020) 7580 1959. *evendine@evendine.com*

Hastings College of Arts & Technology, Archery Road, St Leonards-on-Sea TN38 0HX. Tel: (01424) 442222. Fax: (01424) 721763. e-mail: *reception@hastings.ac.uk www.hastings.ac.uk*
Open University, PO Box 48, Milton Keynes MK7 6HN.
Oxford Business College, *enquiries@oxfordbusinesscollege.co.uk*
Regent Language Training, 14 Buckingham Street, London WC2N 6DF. Tel: (020) 7872 6600. Fax: (020) 7872 6610. *market@regent.org.uk*
UKCOSA, The Council for International Education, 9–17 St Albans Place, London N1 0NX. Tel: (020) 7226 3762. Fax: (020) 7226 3373.

SCHOLARSHIPS

British Council Fellowship Section, The British Council, Medlock Street, Manchester M15 4AA.
The Commonwealth Scholarship Commission, Association of Commonwealth Universities, 36 Gordon Square, London WC1H OPF.
Council for the International Exchange of Scholars, 3007 Tilden Street NW, Suite 5M, Washington DC20008-3009, USA.
Education Department, Overseas Development Administration, 94 Victoria Street, London SW1E 5JL.
The European Commission, Directorate General III, Rue de la Loi 200, B-1049 Brussels, Belgium.

LANGUAGE SCHOOLS

Anglo-Continental, 29-35 Wimborne Road, Bournemouth BH2 6NA. Tel: (01202) 557514. Fax: (01020) 556156. e-mail: *english@anglo-continental.com www.anglo-continental.com*
Bells, Hillscross, Red Cross Lane, Cambridge CB2 0QX. Tel: (01223) 212333. Fax: (01223) 410282. e-mail: *info@bell-schools.ac.uk*
Cicero Languages International, 42 Upper Grosvenor Road, Tunbridge Wells, Kent TN1 2ET. Tel: (01892) 547077. Fax: (01892) 522749. http://www.cicero.co.uk *enrolments@cicero.co.uk*
Concorde International Home Language Tuition, Arnett House, Hawks Lane, Canterbury, Kent CT1 2NU. Tel: (01227) 479279. Fax: (01277) 479379. *www.home-tuition.com info@home-tuition.com*

Eastbourne School of English, 8 Trinity Trees, Eastbourne, East Sussex BN21 3LD. Tel: (01323) 721759. Fax: (01323) 639271. *http://www.esoe.co.uk* e-mail: *english@esoe.co.uk*

Edinburgh School of English, 271 Canongate, The Royal Mile, Edinburgh EH18 8BQ. Tel: (0131) 557 9200. Fax: (0131) 557 9192. *english@edinburghschool.ac.uk*

EF International Language Schools, 1–3 Farman Street, Hove, East Sussex BN3 1AL. Tel: (01273) 201 420. Fax: (01273) 448 566. *ils.uk.agents@ef.com*

Evendine College, 34/36 Oxford Street, London W1D 1AY. Tel: (020) 7636 5656. Fax: (020) 7636 5454. *evendine@evendine.com*

Evendine College, 227/229 Tottenham Court Road, London W1P 9AE. Tel: (020) 7580 1989. Fax: (020) 7580 1959. *evendvine@evendine.com*

InTuition Languages, Kingsmill House, 4 Ravey Street, London EC2A 4QP. Tel: (020) 7739 4411. Fax: (020) 7729 0933. *learn@intuitionlang.com www.intuitionlang.com*

The London School of English, 15 Holland Park Gardens, London W14 8DZ. Tel: (020) 7603 1656. Fax: (020) 7603 5021. *quality@londonschoool.com www.londonschool.com*

Oxford Business College, *enquiries@oxfordbusinesscollege.co.uk*

St Giles College Brighton, 3 Marlborough Place, Brighton BN1 1UB. Tel: (01273) 628274. Fax: (01273) 689808. *stgiles@pavilion.co.uk*

St Giles Colleges Head Office, 154 Southampton Row, Bloomsbury, London WC1B 5JX. Tel: (020) 7837 0404. Fax: (020) 7278 5458. *www.stgiles.co.uk hq@stgiles.co.uk*

St Giles College London Central, 154 Southampton Row, Bloomsbury, London WC1B 5AX. Tel: (020) 7837 0404. Fax: (020) 7837 4099. *london@stgiles.-u-net.com*

St Giles College London Highgate, 51 Shepherds Hill, London N6 5QP. Tel: (020) 8340 0828. Fax: (020) 8348 9389. *lonhigh@stgiles.u-net.com*

Pilgrims Ltd, Pilgrims House, Orchard Street, Canterbury, Kent CT2 8BF. Tel: (01227) 762111. Fax: (01227) 459027. *www.pilgrims.co.uk sales@pilgrims.co.uk*

Regent Language Training, 14 Buckingham Street, London WC2N 6DF. Tel: (020) 7872 6600. Fax: (020) 7882 6610. *market@regent.org.uk*

University of Cambridge Local Examinations Syndicate, Marketing Division, Local Examinations Syndicate, 1 Hills Road, Cambridge CB1 2EU. email: *efl@ucles.org.uk*

EMPLOYMENT

ABC Au Pairs, 42 Underhill Road, Dulwich, London SE22 0QT.
Tel: (020) 8299 3052. Fax: (020) 8299 6086.
vivienne@abc-aupairs.co.uk www.abc-aupairs.co.uk
Little Sprogs, 47 Deane Way, Ruislip, Middx, HA4 8SX. Tel: (020)
8426 1442. *nicola.quinn@littlesprogs.co.uk www.littlesprogs.co.uk*
The London Au Pair & Nanny Agency, Sunnyside, Childs Hill,
Hampstead London NW2 2QN. Tel: (020) 7435 3891. Fax: (020)
7794 2700. *maggie@londonnanny.co.uk*
http://www.londonaupair.co.uk
Nightingale Nannies, Unit 5, 46 Springwood Drive, Braintree,
Essex CM7 9FH. Tel: (01376) 553573.
e-mail: *info@nightingalenannies.co.uk*
Park Lane Nannies, 22 Upper Maudlin Street, Bristol BS2 8DJ. Tel:
(0117) 949 2222. Fax: (0117) 949 2333.
www.parklanenannies.com. park.lane.nannies@cableinet.co.uk
Tinies Childcare, 351 Fulham Palace Road, London SW6 6TB. Tel:
(020) 7384 0322. Fax: (020) 7731 6008.
info@tinieschildcare.co.uk www.tinieschildcare.co.uk

RELIGION

The Baptist Union of Great Britain, Baptist House, PO Box 44, 129
Broadway, Didcot, Oxon OX11 8RT. Tel: (01235) 512077.
e-mail: *baptistuniongb@baptist.org.uk*
The Buddhist Society, 58 Eccleston Square, London SW1V 1PH.
Tel: (020) 7834 5858. Fax: (020) 7976 5238.
http://www.buddsoc.org.uk
Catholic Bishop's Conference, 39 Eccleston Square, London SW1V
1BX.
Church in Wales Centre, Woodland Place, Penarth, Vale of
Glamorgan, Wales CF64 2EX. Tel. (029) 20 7052 78.
CYTUN (Contact for the Majority of religions in Wales) 11 Heol
Sant Helen, Swansea, Wales SA1 4AL. Tel: (01792) 460 876.
The Fellowship of Isis (Goddess worship), Clonegal Castle,
Enniscorthy, Eire (Ireland).
Inter Faith Network for the United Kingdom, 5/7 Tavistock Place,
London WC1H 9SN. Tel: (020) 7388 008. Fax (020) 7387 7968.
e-mail: *ifnet@interfaith.org.uk http:www.interfaith.org.uk*

The Islamic Foundation, Markfield Conference Centre, Ratby Lane, Markfield, Leicestershire LE67 9SY. Tel: (01530) 244944/5. Fax: (01530) 244946.
e-mail: *i.foundation@islamic-foundation.org.uk*
http://www.islamic-foundation.org.uk
The Islamic Centre of England, 140 Maida Vale, London W9 1QP. PO Box 8148, London NW6 7ZS. Tel: (020) 7604 5500. Fax: (020) 7604 4898. e-mail: *icel@icel.org*
National Association of Hindu Temples, 150 Penn Lane, Wolverhampton WV3 0EH.
National Spiritual Assembly of the Baha'is of the United Kingdom, 27 Rutland Gate, London SW7 1PD. Tel: (020) 7584 2566. Fax: (020) 7584 9401. e-mail: *nsa@bahai.org.uk*
http://www.bahai.org.uk
Nederlandse Kerk (Dutch Church), 7 Austin Friars, London EC2N 2EJ.
Norwegian Seamen's Church, St Olav's Square, Albion Street, Rotherhithe, London SE16 1JB. Tel: (020) 7321 0087.
The Pagan Foundation, BM Box 7097, London WC1N 3XX.
e-mail: *secretary@paganfed.demon.co.uk*
Quakers/Religious Society of Friends, 4 Highsett, Hills Road, Cambridge CB2 1NX.
Shree Swaminarayan Temple, 4 Merches Place, Grangetown, Cardiff, Wales CF1 7DR. Tel: (029) 2037 1128.
Union of Muslim Organisations of UK and Eira, 109 Campden Hill Road, London W8 7TL.
United Reformed Church, 86 Tavistock Place, London WC1H 9RT. Tel: (020) 7916 2020. Fax: (020) 7916 2021.
e-mail: *admin@urc.org.uk http://www.urc.org.uk*
United Reform Church/Methodist Church, Persondy, Trallong, Brecon, Powys LD3 8HP.

TRADE COUNCILS AND CHAMBERS OF COMMERCE

Austrian Trade Commission, 45 Prince's Gate, Exhibition Road, London SW7 2QA. Tel: (020) 7584 4411. Fax: (020) 7854 2565.
Belgian-Luxembourg Chamber of Commerce, 8 John Street, London WC1N 2ES. Tel: (020) 7831 3508. Fax: (020) 7831 9151.
Finland Trade Centre, 30–35 Pall Mall, London SW1Y 5LP. Tel: (020) 7747 3000. Fax: (020) 7747 3007.

French Chamber of Commerce, Knightsbridge House, 197 Knights-bridge, London SW7 1RZ. Tel: (020) 7304 4040. Fax: (020) 7304 7034.

Italian Chamber of Commerce, 296 Regent Street, London W1R 5HB. Tel: (020) 7637 3153.

Norwegian British Chamber of Commerce, Norway House, 21/24 Cockspur Street, London SW1Y 5BN. Tel: (020) 7930 0181. Fax: (020) 7930 7946.

Norwegian Trade Council, Charles House, 5–11 Lower Regent Street, London SW1Y 4LR. Tel: (020) 7973 0188. Fax: (020) 7973 0189.

Spanish Chamber of Commerce, 5 Cavendish Square, London W1M 0DP. Tel: (020) 7637 9061.

TRAVEL AND ACCOMMODATION

British Council Arrivals Unit, 10 Spring Gardens, London SW1A 2BN (London area).

British Tourist Authority, 12 Regent Street, London SW1Y 4PQ. Tel: (020) 7499 9325 (hotel accommodation).

Experiment in International Living, 'Otesaga', West Malvern Road, Malvern, Worcestershire, WR14 4EN (homestays with British families).

HOST, 18 Northumberland Avenue, London WC2N 5BJ (home-stays with British families).

International Student House (postal address), 1 Park Crescent, Regent's Park, London W1B 1SH. Entrance address: 229 Great Portland Street, Regent's Park, London W1W 5PN. Tel: (020) 7631 8300. Fax: (020) 7631 8315.
e-mail: *general@ish.org.uk www.ish.org.uk*

London Gatwick Airport general and flight enquiries. Tel: (01293) 535353.

London Hostels Association, 54 Eccleston Square, London SW1V 1PG (student hostels).

Piccadilly Advice Centre, 100 Shaftsbury Avenue, London W1V 7DH (information on hostels).

Student Accommodation Service, 67 Wigmore Street, London W1H 9LG (London area).

Women's Link, 1a Snow Hill Court, London EC1A 2EJ (accom-modation for women in London).

Young Men's Christian Association, 640 Forest Road, London E17 3DZ.

Young Women's Christian Association, 16 Great Russell Street, London WC1B 3LR.

Youth Hostels Association, Trevelyan House, 8 St Stephen's Hill, St Albans, Hertfordshire AL1 2DY (temporary accommodation).

MISCELLANEOUS

Alcoholics Anonymous, PO Box 1, Stonebow House, York YO1 2NJ.

British Broadcasting Corporation, Broadcasting House, London W1A 1AA (for comments, queries or criticism relating to programmes or policy, write to: Viewer and Listener Correspondence, Villiers House, The Broadway, Haven Green, Ealing, London W5 2PA, or phone the Television Information Office on (020) 8743 8000).

Capital Radio London, Euston Tower, Euston Road, London NW1 3DR. Tel: (020) 7608 6080. Fax: (020) 7387 2345.

Greenpeace, Canonbury Villas, London N1 2PN.

Immigration Advisory Service, 2nd Floor, 190 Great Dover Street, London SE1 4YB.

Joint Council for the Welfare of Immigrants, 115 Old Street London EC1V 9JR.

National Association of Citizen's Advice Bureaux, 115 Pentonville Road, London N1 9LZ.

The Vegan Society, Donald Watson House, 7 Battle Road, St Leonards-on-Sea, East Sussex TN37 7AA. Tel: (01424) 427393.

Index